The Truth about Variable Annuities

The Truth

about

Variable Annuities

By

J. Marc Ruggerio, CRC, CWC, FIC

Copyright April 2010 - J. Marc Ruggerio
All rights reserved. No part of this book may be reproduced in any manner whatsoever without written permission of the Author.

ISBN 978-0-557-448-24-1

McGraw-Hill Open Publishing
www.lulu.com

Other Books by J. Marc Ruggerio:

<u>The Truth about R.E.I.T's</u>
(Real Estate Investment Trust's)

The Truth about Variable Annuities

AUTHOR'S DISCLAIMER

The information in this book is for illustration purposes only and should not be relied upon due to the nature of changing products, tax code and regulations. The information herein should not be considered reliable as certain information may have changed as well as been misprinted. While care was taken with regard to the research upon which this information was relied upon, it should not be considered factual and any references made regarding tax code or any other references could have been changed since the printing of this book or the author simply had a senior moment, after all he is human.

The author takes no responsibility and does not guarantee any accuracy of the information provided. The author indemnifies any broker dealer in which he is affiliated with at the time of publishing as well as past and future affiliations. This book and its contents have copyrights but the author will allow reproduction by any person, organization or corporation (entity) to use or quote information provided herein as long as that information is not reproduced in a biased or negative manner, that such reproduction does not state it is guaranteed, reliable or considered factual and the author has been informed in writing and granted such person or entity written permission prior to utilization of the books contents. The author is not engaged in selling securities, nor is securities offered/presented/ recommended for purchase by the author. The material covered in this book should be considered the authors opinion and not advice or recommendation.

The Truth about Variable Annuities

The Truth about Variable Annuities

This book is dedicated to my wife and best friend, Ann Marie, for always being there, through good and bad times, always remaining positive and supportive. Without you I would still be cleaning carpets or bagging groceries!

To my dad, I would like to thank for introducing me to the business and always looking out for me.

To my children, I want you to know anything is possible if you set your mind to it. And remember, there is no "try", only "do". It is always best to have tried and failed than to have never tried! Always be prepared for an opportunity!

The Truth about Variable Annuities

Table of Contents

Authors Disclaimer	Page 4
Intro: The Purge Valve	Page 9
I: Understanding Owner /Annuitant Driven	Page 40
II: The Contract Owner	Page 58
III: The Annuitant	Page 81
IV: The Beneficiary	Page 87
V: Death Benefits	Page 94
VI: Living Benefits	Page 100
VII: Pro-Rata vs. 4	Page 106
VIII: Authors Note	Page 118
IX: Compliance & Exchanges	Page 126
X: Annuity Worksheet	Page 136
XI: Truth about Step up's	Page 137
XII: Expert Strategies	Page 143
XIII: Illustrating the Structure	Page 155
XIV: Final Thoughts	Page 167

Introduction:

The Purge Valve

I decided to write this book in hopes it would allow for more financial advisors, attorneys, policy holders and other advisors a simple and effective means of learning more about such a complex product that can be extremely beneficial as part of an overall financial plan.

In many cases throughout my many years of speaking and training financial advisors across the nation, I have been asked numerous times to review old annuity policies. Sadly, these annuities I reviewed were often the only asset that remained to support the client in retirement. More than often annuities end up the primary means of "income survival" outside of Social Security, that Americans have come to depend on for the bulk of their retirement. What is disturbing is that compliance, companies and regulators alike try and dictate the amount and use of an individual's percentage allocated to the one investment that will provide them a lifetime of income. Think about it for a moment using common sense, if a person has only a few assets that will provide barely enough to survive on during retirement why would they want to take risk to that income? Being forced to use a diversified approach that would not protect a guaranteed lifetime income does not make sense to me. If an investment allows me to take the same risk and attain the potential same return as an allocation/investment that is not going to guarantee income, why would I choose the non-guaranteed one? It has nothing to do with over-zealous salespeople, commission vs. fee, or greed. It has everything to do with doing what is best for the client.

The only other 2 options would be to remain in a purely guaranteed investment that would allow the client to go broke safely and allow inflation to terrorize their income and lifestyle daily until they become poverty stricken. Or, they could follow the "rules" of firms, companies and regulators and take on all the risk by allowing an advisor to "diversify" them in a managed account or other investments that cannot provide a guaranteed income for life. All this strategy "could" do is provide a return and allow the client to "hope" that it provided enough of a return to sustain them during their entire retirement. Buying a lotto ticket with your last dollar and "hoping" is probably not the smartest thing to do nor does it make for a good strategy. Well, I think we all agree "hope' is not a strategy. I cannot recall how many times I have heard the following statement from a policy holders lips in a meeting but it was one too many to ignore and struck a chord deep within me and encouraged me to write this book; (summarized from years of hearing similar iterations)

"I bought that annuity because some saleswoman strong-armed me into buying it (or an old friend got in the insurance business). I was upset with them for many years because all I heard was how bad annuities were. I hated *thinking I got ripped off. I never told anyone about this annuity because I thought it made me look stupid. Many years I had regretted buying it. I didn't understand the annuity then and I remain dumbfounded today. Now, after learning more about my annuity and looking back, it may be one of the smartest financial decisions I didn't know I made. Without this guarantee and the income provided I wouldn't know what I would do to make ends meet. I just wish I had gotten my advisors to review it and help manage it before now. Nobody ever discusses all the things we have just reviewed, you should write a book!"*

And now you know the whole story of how this book came to fruition. I have tried to bring attention to and provide clear examples of many areas of variable annuities throughout this book. Since many companies literature, marketing material or printed material, will not clearly state if the contract is "owner" or "annuitant driven" I wanted to start here first. Unless you understand the subject of Contract Structuring Annuities and can read and comprehend a prospectus, should you be able to identify if a contract is "owner or annuitant driven". Many financial advisors I have met in the last 15 years do not fully understanding how to <u>properly</u> structure an annuity, all the taxation issues, the numerous distribution options or how the thousands of living/death benefit features actually work.

To truly comprehend all the ramifications of combining income guarantees and death benefits takes time and effort. Combining them could be detrimental or fortuitous to their client in certain situations. When you understand all the issues advisors have on their plates running a business, managing assets, dealing with client emotions, staying in compliance and fearing the regulators I often wonder how they remain sane! They have to understand, comprehend and retain enough knowledge always in order to avoid mistakes that could cost them their license or career! Next, they have to worry about staying in business and then once they have achieved enough education and built up a good practice can they truly allow themselves the time to concentrate on a few areas they want to pursue a deeper understanding. That is why many financial advisors are literally broke until several years of building a practice. One thing I would like to clarify is the money (income/net worth) of most financial advisors typically comes after 12-15 years of building a practice.

Most advisors have paid a steep financial price to finally gain their own financial stability. The knowledge and experience they attain over this period is nowhere to be found in the normal methods advisors use to learn. Sure, today you can get a degree and read some books but that does not make an advisor. We all know what works in the classroom rarely succeeds in the real world! Continuing Education today has become the joke of the industry as it is nothing more than a requirement and nobody really learns or continues their education. Few can utilize the opportunity to learn something new, while most advisors are guilty of just "getting it over with" by finding a subject they are already experts in just to satisfy the annual credits to keep their license. You cannot blame them as they are very busy trying to keep their clients focused on the long term plan and not the short term emotions of the market.

It is not the advisors fault that very little material or information is available on such complicated subjects like contract structure. Due to the limited availability of this information I chose to write this book in order to help clients and advisors have a basic foundation and understanding of some of the things to think about when purchasing an annuity.

I have also been asked by many to bring things out in the open that no one wants to talk about or directly face. So, I have addressed a few of these main issues to specific parties below as well as throughout this book. Some of these issues are always there, but like some type of taboo subject matter, no one will actually say the words or bring out in the open. We all just deal with the effects to no avail. Getting some of these issues out and making it known how all parties feel may further the entire industry and launch these relationships into the future. Get prepared, as I have touched on many issues that will make some feel uneasy while reading in such a direct manner. Below you will read in a very blunt manner some of the most important issues no one wants to hear out loud. This is your chance to learn and contemplate these issues. It is important to understand others viewpoints in order to succeed at anything. Here are a few pointers that were the most common denominators addressed to each group; Clients, Advisors and Wholesalers.

For Clients

If you are an investor that abhors annuities and will not even discuss them with your advisor, shame on you for being closed minded! I have just one question for you that you can answer; "Where did you attain your great knowledge that you possess which affords you the opportunity to so confidently shun variable annuities?" Let me guess, your friend, mechanic, family member, plumber, cashier at the grocery store, accountant or someone that knows nothing about nothing told you to stay away from annuities and since you trust them you have shunned annuities all these years. Well, my friend, if you are reading this book I hope it will enlighten you enough to open your investment mind to listen and learn more before making decisions! Mostly I hope that it teaches you that while trust is a very important factor, trust itself is not in question here. It is the knowledge behind that trust that you must trust. You can always trust a person, but you have the right to not trust their opinion or attain a second opinion!

If you own an annuity and have a basic structure where one person is the owner and the annuitant and the spouse is the beneficiary you may have a structure that very basic and should or could be amended to provide more benefits to avoiding costly future issues. Not that it is a bad structure, but you could change your current structure to allow some wiggle room for issues that you may face in the future. In many cases you can change your structure even if it has been years since you have originally bought it. I suggest you revisit with your advisor and ask them about it. If the advisor does not have the expertise simply ask them if they have others they turn to for assistance in these types of complicated issues. As a last resort you may want to search out someone that truly understands annuities. Sometimes the best financial advisors are forced to sell a product or take over an asset they know little about due to the client bringing it with their portfolio. Again, many annuities may have been bought just to buy something and not truly part of a financial plan. This is probably how 80% of all annuities are issued. So, do not fault your advisor for not knowing everything about your current annuity when you ask them to review it.

In many cases even an expert would need time to review and get the appropriate questions answered over a 30 day period to provide proper information and plan accordingly. The key takeaway here is to talk openly and ask questions to your trusted advisor. They are there to help you. You just need to ask! Call your advisor tomorrow, get to know them more on a personal level and start learning more about your own investments as well!

For Advisors

The next time you have a wholesaler discuss a company product with you, try finding out more about the wholesaler and how they can help you truly understand their product before discussing the features and benefits. Making sure your wholesaler is experienced, knowledgeable, and will be around to assist you long into the future is the key to a trusting relationship. Knowing they come highly referred and regarded by others (your peers and competitors) is another way to judge their abilities. Just because one product offers your client a 6% guarantee and the other a 5% guarantee, does not mean it is better. I can spend hours showing and proving how 5% is much better than 6% in numerous situations-not using "funny" math either.

Knowing your clients situation and potential future issues they may face is the starting point to properly placing your client's funds in the right annuity. The company ratings, benefits/features, cost and support should be second to the structure. First, find the right type of annuity (owner/annuitant driven) then find the top rated, least costly, best wholesaler, and finally remain objective and unbiased. Who cares if one company has better marketing, is larger, better name recognition, and has a cuter mascot or better trinkets for your desk? Have you ever heard the phrase, "too big to fail?" Yeah, me too! Your clients depend on you to be unbiased and remain focused on their individual circumstance. Getting into the habit of using one company's annuity/feature/benefit is the beginning of your end. Complacency is never a good thing.

One last thing, many wholesalers have asked me to address some key issues. These issues that are discussed below were the most common denominator that seemed to hold back greatness. These issues have needed a purge value for a long time. These next few pages will be that purge value for advisors and wholesalers. I had decidedly chosen to not candy-coat these sections. <u>But I ask you to do me a favor, don't shoot the messenger.</u> Here goes:

These most common wholesaler requests were that upon your next wholesaler appointment to please be prepared for the meeting. In many cases the wholesaler has spent at least an hour researching you and your business in order to provide you with value in that 30 minute meeting. They have searched you on the internet, viewed your U-4 on FINRA.org, viewed your company website and most likely already asked about you from others in the area, other wholesalers (yes wholesalers are competitors but they know how to keep their enemies closer than friends) or may have been referred to you. They are often away from their family at length and Marriott is their first home. They went through literal hell to reach you. Trains, planes, rental cars, bad cell connections, lazy internet speed, misplaced reservations, bad and mostly unhealthy dieting, and very long hours. They typically wake at 6am and hit the bed at midnight after traveling an average of 200 miles per day. They work in a circle over an entire area in four days then deal with airline security.

You owe it to them, to yourself and your clients to have a notepad ready to take all their information and great ideas down. They have intimate knowledge of the top firms, products and advisors and see firsthand the most successful and biggest advisor failures. Have some questions ready. Give them a shot at adding value to your business.

DO NOT ASK THEM HOW THEIR RIDER COMPETES WITH THE ONE YOU ARE COMPLACENT WITH! Wholesalers can see the red-stains on your kool-aid lips from drinking at your "complacent annuity" company's trough. If you really want to see a great wholesalers value take your biased hat off and allow both of you to have a no holds barred conversation of what each of you think or feel. Taking the gloves off will reveal a lot. Allowing this openness about products, features/benefits, costs and the good/bad/ugly will be an experience you will never forget! Allow the wholesaler to truly explain why they feel your "complacent annuity" is inferior/superior. Getting many opinions you will start to see a common denominator from many different sources. I have learned when many different sources begin having a common denominator I better pay attention. Allow them to show their value and provide you the niche of where their product fits. If you have core and niche products you have all the gaps filled. Allow them the opportunity to compete at some level, core or niche, but allow them to compete!

Many advisors do not feel wholesalers can bring them value. Have you thought that maybe you've not been open to learning about how they can bring value? Are you truly allowing them the opportunity to show their value? Were you paying attention to what they were saying when you met with them, or were you thinking of a really good question about the complacent product you utilize for every client in order to just get the wholesaler to leave and not come back (my 6% beats your 5%)? Or, were you staring into your computer screen watching those mesmerizing little green/red colors like a kid on Saturday morning cartoons? Those stocks you are watching, you and I know are not in need of seeing every uptick or downtick. Quit ignoring the professional sitting with you knee-cap to knee-cap and quit making excuses.

Talking about how much you love your "complacent annuity" and its features is a complete waste of the wholesaler's time. They know more about *your* annuity than you do. You will not teach them anything. Their company has a complete department dedicated to learning the *competition. Every small detail on your annuity is sitting on a report in the wholesaler's briefcase mere inches from you that the wholesaler has memorized! The wholesaler probably already reviewed it in your parking lot because he knows which product you are using.*

Most wholesalers have years of training and experience with numerous designations, are expert public speakers and on top of their game. They take their profession just as serious as you take yours. Give them that! The smartest and most successful advisors I know and have worked with understand this and want to extract everything they can from their wholesalers brains! Finding those key wholesalers that you can rely on because they have many years of experience and much knowledge on such things can be an asset to you. I personally would want to be expert in a few things rather than attain basic knowledge on many things. Years ago I was given some really good advice, "become an expert (or at least really good) at one thing during your life because nobody likes a know-it-all—literally having the ability to comment on everything because you know a little about everything makes you look like a jerk". *Are you* challenging your wholesaler to make you the best, to give you all they have to offer? They may be the key to allowing you significant success and avoid costly litigation, compliance or regulatory challenges. Find that great wholesaler, befriend them, partner with them and everyone benefits; you, them and your clients! I challenge you, to challenge your wholesaler, starting immediately! Are you prepared?

For Wholesalers

(For those that do not know what a wholesaler is: A wholesaler is a term used to describe the Regional Vice President of a company and are charged with distributing their company products to the financial advisors and the financial planning firms. They are supposed to be the experts on the product and should educate others on their products proper positioning and utilization.) I have asked numerous financial advisors all over the country for some issues relating to wholesalers. I have also spoken with insurance company executives and managers of wholesalers to point out important wholesaler/advisor issues and help relay some messages here as well. The days of wholesaling by running around seeing financial advisors to pitch your 6%

beats their 5% are over. The golf days and dinner nights are not something that was never considered the best use of time. In today's world of muted benefits, more complex products, advisors increased knowledge, insurance company legacy asset risk, IXI data, extreme databases, GPS, and significant ways to measure effectiveness you better bring your value and bring it quick. There are huge numbers of very talented people waiting on the sidelines for the opportunity you have. Ask yourself the 2 main questions:

- What value can I bring to an advisor?
- What value is this particular advisor looking for me to bring to them?

Your days are very limited if you think you can remain at a company for years being mediocre, playing golf with your best advisors, taking new advisors to dinner, or relying on your company to provide you the perceived "best" benefit (6% beats 5%). You must fully understand your own annuity and ALL ramifications and then know your competition even better. Not bashing your competitor, but knowing more about their product than their own wholesaler will immediately set you apart. Providing the advisor with true value, some pointers, specific questions or knowledge about their current "complacent annuity" they are using will allow for them to test you while they learn something about their "complacent annuity". They are complacent because they have become comfortable with it. They may have spent significant time performing due diligence and getting to know the wholesaler.

Don't blindly assume advisors are using their complacent annuity for no reason. Remember, advisors lives are just as hard as yours due to the fact they are dealing with employees, clients, regulators, compliance and their own personal families. Maybe their wholesaler is such an expert they could run circles around your best efforts. Maybe they are complacent because they don't know how to learn a new annuity. You owe it to them to be fully prepared and have done your research to make that appointment valuable to them, yourself, and the company you represent. Fight the good fight.

Understand the advisor and their business before throwing up on their desk your product feature and benefits.

Who cares about your widget or step-up feature if your company's pre-emptive structuring language won't fit the advisors business model? Ask the right questions, and you may find a great opportunity and reason to prove your value to the advisor. They may become interested and learn something and you begin to help the advisor with their clients and attain sales. In short, be on top of your game, know your stuff cold, and "bring it" often. My personal motto for years has been, "Make dust, don't eat it." You may recall a certain funny movie that had a quote in it, "If you ain't first, you're last." There is no second place in a two-man race, no matter what your mommy told you. Don't go counting your blue ribbons when everyone got a blue ribbon just for showing up...... Now, Man-Up and compete at the highest level.

Is there anyone else that needed a pep talk? Any more issues hiding just under the surface that needed a purge valve? Gosh, I hope not. That was not fun for me. Yup, sometimes the truth hurts but can set you free. I hope all you advisors and wholesalers are happy now that issues like these have a voice and can now be addressed……so let's get back to the book.

To help you understand all the moving parts and be able to also clearly become witness to the truth about variable annuities, I have broken the book into chapters that only speak to certain issues, parties, benefits or conceptual illustrations. This allows you to clearly and quickly review specific issues as needed and to gain a better understanding of what to ask. I wanted to build a book that was meant for review but also clearly provided the ability to help someone fully understand the issues and not walk away dumbfounded. I have also tried to keep the "entertainment" aspect to a minimum, although I sometimes got bored and needed to add a laugh here or there.

I can honestly say that over the last 15 years I have yet to find a true situation where an annuity was sold to someone with the clear intent to hurt them. They are complex and that complexity is often taken advantage of by the client's "selective memory" or the attorney representing the client, not wanting to "confuse the facts with a good story". While someone might point to the fact the advisor is licensed, we all know what this means, they simply passed a test. Many financial planners do not sell variable annuities and will accommodate their client only when the client approaches them and are about to buy it from someone else. **Many clients find out about annuities from other places and not their own advisor! This is the root of the problem.** Some financial advisors, firms and even clients feel annuities have a "taboo" or negative stigma attached so they avoid selling them, buying them or educating their clients or themselves out of fear they look like commission hungry salesmen. The average commission of variable annuities today is the same or less than mutual funds. You never hear negatives or how the high compensation of mutual funds compromised advisors integrity.

Let me set the record straight here and now. Ask yourself if you would deliberately sell a product for a small commission and maybe after taxes/expenses take home enough to pay the mortgage for one month jeopardize your career and your family's well-being for that one sale? Yeah, when you think about it nobody would. But attorneys won't let the facts get in the way of a good story, eh? Many advisors have spent their entire life dedicated to their profession just as a doctor does. As "Financial Doctors", they have similar integrity and numerous laws to follow. They make a decent living and 99.99% would not jeopardize that for one small annuity where they may make after taxes and expenses one mortgage payment or grocery bill. I can tell you some of the most wealthy and brightest individuals and advisors I know have used variable annuities at a very high level with clients for many years. The cases I have seen would blow your mind! Some of these clients are worth many hundreds of millions of dollars and their advisors the brightest in the industry.

One other issue is the fee planner or (RIA) Registered Investment Advisor that is not associated with a FINRA Broker Dealer. These types of advisors often times only charge a fee for advice or an ongoing fee to manage your assets within financial products. However, they do not have the ability to sell certain products even if they are licensed as some products only allow for a commission and they only accept a fee. The fee/commission debate has been around an awful long time and I would like to end it here and now. Just like guns do not kill people, people kill people; the commission or the fee is not the problem/answer, it is the perception of the advisor!

So, if someone tells you an advisor is better because they charge fees or commission I beg you to run away, run fast! That argument is nothing more than a sales pitch! Think about this for a moment. A fee planner has a vested interest in making sure the client is taken care of and the advisor acts in a fiduciary capacity. The commission advisor has a vested interest in the client after the commission as they need to manage the product performance/relationship and acts in a financial relationship capacity.

Actually, if you were to look at the industry commissions on a nationwide basis you would find the average annuity commission is much lower that mutual funds and most advisors opt to take a lower commission that offers a trail fee/commission that is very similar to the fee planner. I would guess (based on my 15 years) that over half of all advisors take a trail option commission (1%) and when you look at the taxes, expenses, and firm fees and payouts the advisor's net take home for selling an annuity is paltry. With the average annuity sale under $60,000 I will allow you to do the math. When you hear that advisors are "getting rich selling variable annuities" now you may have some insight and question for those making that statement. You may even want to ask them why they are so intent on stating that!

Back to the fee vs. commission; so, if both types of advisors have ongoing interest for their client and the investment and both are getting paid an ongoing revenue stream, I ask you to decide who is better? Yeah, the truth and facts make things a little clearer and much harder to defend a position, eh? Both must take care of their clients in an ongoing manner and in hopes of new business in the form of new assets or by referral. Crooks and bad people are out there but a commission or fee makes neither! Bad people will be bad, there is no stopping that. But to deem someone good or bad by the way they want to run their business is elementary, shows a low level of thought and is obviously biased.

In short, find the advisor you can trust. I don't mean the kind of trust concerning them stealing your money, that is obvious, but the kind that you trust in their expertise and knowledge and knowing they will do what they say they will. DO NOT LET YEARS OF EXPERIENCE FORM YOUR OPINION! I personally know many advisors that have 30 years "experience". But in truth some have the same one year experience, 30 times! They never continued to learn or be a student of the business, but instead found that they were a great "asset gatherer" or salesperson and did that for the last 30 years; gathered assets and made fees or commissions. I personally want a firm that has 2 types of partners. The first being the "people partner" and the second being the no personality "nerd". That equates to a great team that will succeed. The "people partner" will gather enough assets to keep the firm running and more successful to remain in business. The "nerd" will continue their education and perform at the highest levels. Many of these firms will eventually add a team of analyst to assist them as well. One easy way to grade your advisor is ask yourself this question: How many times has my advisor asked me to come in to specifically show me a new product that I currently do not own? I don't mean taking your XYZ Mutual Fund and moving to ABC Mutual Fund. I am talking about selling a portion of your stock position or portfolio to buy or reallocate to something that fits the portfolio like REIT's or oil/gas, or something very different due to the direct affect it will have on the overall portfolio and financial plan as a whole for the end result.

Under normal circumstances this could be a clear indication your advisor is continuing to learn and be a student of the business. If the new investment clearly makes sense for you as it relates to your overall portfolio and your overall plan, then you have a great advisor! If you have an advisor that just performs annual reviews and doesn't contact you much, they are happy making their fee and just don't want to offer you the opportunity to get upset and leave and take their fee revenue with you! Finally, I would want my annuity advisor that sells at least $5 million of Variable Annuities per year and even more if you add fixed annuities. This would indication a level of success and sophistication as the firm would have to manage a significant amount of these types of assets in just a few short years. They would also have company wholesalers calling on them and educating them in hopes of attaining their business. They would have access to the annuity company's best and brightest in the industry. They would be much sharper than someone with only a handful of annuity clients.

Speaking of insurance company's representatives, you should ask your advisor if he works closely with them. If they are brought in on the appointments with clients this also shows trust between them as well. Knowing how long the advisor and "wholesaler" have been working together is a clear and precise indication of expertise and trust factors. How long has the "wholesaler" been in that role? Indications of highly successful wholesalers are the longevity at company(s) and if they have been in the same geographical territory for many years. They have reputations to uphold and word spreads like lightening for bad wholesalers. Seeing wholesalers that move all over the country with many different companies (especially if they are young and single) is something to consider. They may look great and speak well, but in reality they may not have loyalty to the company/territory and will leave when something else they want is presented.

    I have also found clients and advisors to act very similar when it comes to meetings. Clients typically show up for a review with no notepad or pen. Most just sit for an hour and listen to a bunch of talk about the performance of the portfolio and then what changes the advisor is proposing. These proposed changes often allow the advisor a new fee/commission or there may be trading cost associated with proposed changes but mostly they are a necessity to update a portfolio. Clients should be prepared for the meeting with very general and specific questions as it relates to why things are changing and it must make sense. You should be prepared to ask questions. These questions should be related to making sure there is a benefit and ongoing benefit to you and always challenge the advisor to help educate you by asking questions that allow you to better comprehend your portfolio more clearly. Many times this allows you to find out how knowledgeable the advisor is in what they are proposing. They will not know every detail but good advisors will know 95%. Trust this advisor! Be fully prepared for all meetings!

With these few pointers I hope this book offers you the value of knowledge in such a complex product. I hope you have prepared to learn very complex but intriguing things about variable annuities that you never knew! Finally, you may learn the "truth" about annuities. Enjoy.

Chapter I

Understanding Owner and Annuitant Driven Annuities

An Annuity is a contract between the annuity owner and the issuing insurance company. An Annuity is only offered through Insurance Company's under IRS guidelines. The (PAT) Private Annuity Trust has come under IRS scrutiny of late and they are more complex and may not be worth the liability. <u>There are always 3 parties involved in an Annuity: Owner, Annuitant, and Beneficiary</u>. These parties can have multiple (joint) parties or sub parties (contingent) as well. In many cases they can be the same party as well. Later, I will define and explain the roles of each interested party within the annuity contract. The fact that the owner, annuitant, and beneficiary provisions vary from company-to-company and contract-to-contract can really complicate the matter. Only by knowing the contract in question can you determine the rights and benefits that pertain to the parties involved in the annuity. In many cases insurance companies have written in "blanket or pre-emptive" language to their contracts or prospectuses as a means of protecting their policyholder from unexpected consequences. It is very important to know some of these pre-emptive clauses prior to purchasing an annuity from a company if your financial plan is complex or requires very specific attention in regards to distributing assets to heirs or your estate.

In order to fully understand all the information in this book you must first understand what makes an annuity pay a 1) Death Benefit, 2) Enhanced Death Benefit or 3) Distribution. Annuities are either *Owner* **or** *Annuitant* 'Driven". In rare cases, a contract may be both *Owner* **and** *Annuitant* Driven depending on the contract. If that is the case, particular attention must be made to follow IRS guidelines and regulations as well as company rules pertaining to distribution or death benefits.

Believe it or not, death is not the only reason for an annuity to pay out a distribution, nor is it a pre-requisite. First, you need to know if the contract is "Owner" or "Annuitant" driven before you can assess the multiple scenarios under which distributions may occur. Insurance companies build their annuity death benefit but IRS regulations must be adhered to always. The IRS regulations require that, with any annuity, whether "owner driven" or "annuitant driven", if an <u>owner dies</u>, the *value** of the contract must be distributed to the primary beneficiary under Section 72 of the Internal Revenue Code. *(*Value is determined by the annuity contract and under what scenario distributions occur or benefits utilized).* However, if the annuitant dies in an "owner driven" contract (as long as the annuitant is not also the owner or co-owner), the contract will remain in force and a new annuitant can be named or the contingent or co-annuitant becomes the new annuitant. There is only one exception to this rule under IRC Section 72 (S). This clause specifically addresses the spousal exemption rule. It is very clear in that the "spouse of a deceased owner, being named the sole primary beneficiary, may continue a contract and becomes the new owner." Now, this is where it gets complex, as sometimes there may be joint owners of the annuity and the spouse of one of the owners is named as primary (sole) beneficiary. *(See example A below)* An owner has died and therefore under IRC 72s rules, a death benefit distribution must occur. However, the pre-emptive clauses by some companies state that the remaining living joint owner supersedes the beneficiary and now becomes the primary beneficiary, complicating the issues and possibly causing lawsuits by heirs or estates. As you can see this is only one example of how important it is to fully understand the contract, the company and all IRS regulations as it relates to the specific annuity BEFORE PURCHASING! <u>All cases or illustrations in this</u>

book assume that death occurs prior to the annuity start date unless clearly noted. *Value can be determined many different ways as you will see in this book.

Example A:

John and his brother Tom are the owners of a variable annuity with deposits of $100,000 due to a business arrangement. John's wife Stacy is the primary and sole beneficiary. The annuitant must be John or Tom in order to avoid what we commonly refer to as "The Unholy Trinity". Having 3 separate parties to a contract has very negative IRS consequences. To avoid this Tom or John can be named the annuitant. Let's assume John is the annuitant. If the contract were an annuitant driven policy and the death benefit is $300,000 but the current value is $200,000 and John (the annuitant) dies, Stacy (the beneficiary) would receive the enhanced death benefit ($300,000). However, Tom (an owner) is still alive. This poses a problem as Tom is the "taxable entity" according to the IRS. So, in this example Tom may owe income taxes on the gain ($200,000) and possible gift taxes beyond the exclusion limit and worst of all, tom may also owe the 10% excise tax on the gain as well (penalty IRC Section 72q) if he is under 59 ½ years old. However, if the company has "blanket or pre-emptive" language that supersedes this outcome by allowing Tom to become the annuitant it all works out if that were the intended consequences. Yet, the intention may have been the former for business purposes and now those plans were foiled due to the insurance companies' language that is in force as a means of "helping". These are good intentions and generally work well but as long as they are known to all parties and financial advisors mistakes can be avoided!

Now that I have completely confused you let me explain what "owner" or "annuitant driven" means. When speaking of "driven" it refers to how, when and what the insurance company will pay. Sometimes their policy is directly conflicting with IRS rules and therefore the IRS rules will be followed, sometimes to the detriment of the beneficiary as it relates to "value". In short, if a contract is "owner driven" the death benefit will pay out proceeds to the beneficiary "upon death of the owner". In some cases, due to tax law, the death benefit will pay out proceeds to the beneficiary upon a contractual change of the owner. An example would be if Dad is the owner of his own existing deferred annuity, then changes ownership of his annuity to his adult Son. Some tax authorities have claimed that if Dad did give his annuity to his son by changing the ownership, Dad would owe the income tax on the gain or untaxed portion, possible gift tax of the entire annuity beyond the gift limit, and a possible 10% IRS penalty on the gain within the contract if Dad were under age 59 ½. Others have also claimed that the son receiving such a gift may also be held liable for certain taxes as well. Welcome to the wonderful world of IRS subjective interpretation! If a contract is "annuitant-driven", upon the death of the annuitant, the death benefit will pay out to the beneficiary. *CAUTION! Some companies will only pay a death benefit after the second annuitant's death if the* contract has joint or co-annuitants. As you can see you should choose your Annuitants wisely! You may not want the annuity to payout anytime soon, so you could make great grandmother (age 85) and your daughter (age 25) the annuitants! Death benefits vary as well, depending on what the prospectus says. If the death benefit is payable upon the death of the annuitant and the owner is changed, the IRS mandates payout/distribution to the beneficiary. But if this were to occur the distribution may be the contract value which may be less than the actual death benefit.

FOR EXAMPLE:

Regarding a change in ownership, what would the payout be in an "annuitant driven" contact if the contract value is $200,000 and the death benefit is $300,000? (Technically, you must read the prospectus under death benefits for the answer.) The enhanced death benefit would be $300,000 if the annuitant died; yet the owner was changed (or has died) and distribution must now occur due to IRS guidelines. The distribution could only be $200,000 since the contract was "annuitant driven" but the owner was changed or died and the IRS mandates a distribution upon the owner change or death of the owner! The tax scenario of Dad giving Son his annuity is played out here, as well as the loss of the $100,000 enhanced death benefit since the contract is no longer in existence. Can you say lawsuit? If you didn't notice, there is a big difference between "death benefit" and "Enhanced death benefit" or distribution. You must pay very close attention to these words and sentences; they have significantly different meaning sometimes.

To figure out the structure of the annuity contract you need the prospectus. I would also suggest writing the company and asking for the SAI (Statement of Additional Information). This also will allow for more information. Find the section in the prospectus that details the death benefit. It should read clearly whose death triggers a death benefit or enhanced death benefit. There is other confusing language here regarding the actual death benefit. Remember to read over The Death Benefit and The Living Benefit chapters. These chapters will explain "Dollar for Dollar" and "pro-rata" withdrawals and the affects each have on death benefits and living benefits. *Caution! Some contracts allow the death benefit to be affected by withdrawals on a Dollar for Dollar basis, but at the same time allow the Living Benefit to be affected by withdrawals on a pro-rata basis! Financial Advisors must know their client, their needs and the annuity contract! I feel it is the Financial Advisor's responsibility to fully understand the structure of the annuity they sell and its impact on their clients. They are licensed to sell Annuities, yet, I have never met an Advisor that has been trained on this subject outside of continuing education classes! While most advisors keep the structure simple and it works 80% of the time for all clients, there are many cases where it could be shown there would have been greater policy benefits if the advisor fully understood contract structuring. Knowing the client and their intentions, as well as all the annuity provisions and benefits can add additional value to a financial plan when utilizing annuities.*

You will find examples of structuring throughout this book to help you understand the many reasons for simple and complex annuity structures. Trusts and estate planning, as well as divorce, play an important role in the structuring of annuities. (In the United States, I have often heard that roughly 54% of all marriages end in divorce.) This leaves children, stepchildren, grandchildren, and step-grandchildren all as potential heirs. Imagine structuring an annuity where the stepchildren should only be paid as beneficiaries if the natural children are deceased (contingent beneficiaries). You must know exactly how to structure the annuity in case an owner or annuitant dies. Not to mention the affects structuring will have on estate planning and possible ownership changes and how it could affect the beneficiary payout to natural or stepchildren in cases of another divorce. Look at every available scenario with regard to stock market fluctuations, withdrawals, and contract guarantees, and then choose the structure wisely. I personally have always had an eye towards what I call the "Teflon Coat" approach to structuring. I have always tried to think through every scenario that may affect the annuity and find the one structure that can achieve the most benefit in all those scenarios. In many cases annuity owners have no need for complex structuring until much later. That is why it is so important to initiate a structure with an eye for the future. I have seen 35 year marriages fall apart, accidental death, and complex business arrangements that a simple knowledge of structuring could have fixed in the very beginning. In many cases rather than naming the husband as owner and annuitant with the spouse as sole primary beneficiary, adding a little more can go a long way. If naming husband and spouse as joint owners and designating the beneficiary as "the surviving joint owner/spouse" can fix many future problems. This allows for either spouse to die and be able to take advantage of spousal continuation.

There is a paradox in the search for reliable information. Certified Public Accountants, Attorneys, and Financial Planners are the first place to look for help with structuring an annuity contract. However, they may be the only place to look as well. There are few people in the United

States that understand this subject fully. Finding them will be laborious. You may get lucky with a Tax Attorney. I would hate to see their fees, especially if annuity structure is not their specialty. Remember, just because someone is licensed does not mean they are competent; they just happened to be able to pass the test or other requirements. Having a financial advisor that understands their weaknesses and has relationships with other experts or resources, allows for the best opportunity to get accurate information and help with your structuring needs. However, many advisors do not have a firm enough foundation to know there is such a thing a complex structuring. It will be up to you to assess and aggress whether an advisor is capable of helping you or referring you to the right person.

Financial Planners with back office resources may be the best hope for proper structuring information. Some of the Advisor firms have back offices that help in this area. They also have access to the company that provides the annuity. Most of these Insurance Companies have Advanced Planning departments or Legal Departments regarding their product. However, few are willing to become liable for any structuring so they do not like to discuss this topic. They can offer general advice but nothing specifically. They will always refer the Advisor or client to their own CPA or Attorney. Now we are back to square one! The company will give all the relevant information needed to properly structure the annuity offered by their company but they rarely comment on the structure.

There is one company based in Chicago, Illinois that previously specialized in structuring of annuities. They have morphed into a different type of company and also changed their name to Advanced Sales Corporation (ASC) which allows Financial Advisors or firms (Broker Dealers) to pay a fee for access to a database that houses most variable annuities (indexed annuities also). This database allows for an advisor to attain significant information on each annuity with very specific details of the structure, rider, costs, and much more. ASC is the only firm in the nation that is currently assisting the largest firms and thousands of advisors with such detailed and helpful information. This detailed information being immediately available to an advisor for comparison and research is tremendously valuable! Their "Annuity Intelligence Report" allows an advisor a comprehensive tool that provides a wealth of information on numerous variable annuities in a very user-friendly format. The advisor can uncover particular strengths and weaknesses of a proposed annuity "before" the sale! The advisor has the ability to get quick and accurate answers to their annuity questions or research comparatives issues.

Having an advisor that represents a firm that is supported with this information means they will have the necessary information to assist you in annuity planning.

Another structuring idea:

This example is fairly straight forward and easy to understand but what are not illustrated are the numerous issues to be considered to make the planned outcome become a reality. Having it work smoothly takes significant effort and know-how. Imagine if you had the opportunity to invest in something that grows and would lock in at the highest point no matter what happens in the future. Say you invested $100,000 and you are age 30. That investment over a few years grew to $300,000 and then it lost money and went back down to $200,000. Wouldn't it be nice to take a time machine back to when the value was $300,000 and cash in before the losses occurred? Well, the variable annuity may be your time machine in this example. Imagine, at age 30 with a high tolerance of investment risk you invested $100,000 in a variable annuity and allocated it all to the technology fund in 1998. We all know what happened in 1998 to 2000. Huge gains were made! Then the technology crash! You topped out a gain of $300,000 and then losses made your account currently worth $200,000. If you are the owner of the annuity, made your 76 year old relative or friend the annuitant in an annuitant driven policy, and you were the primary sole beneficiary you could win big in this example. If your age 76 friend (annuitant) were in bad health and you felt fairly sure they would pre-decease you (this is a significant issue by the way) this works to your advantage. Assume 5 years has passed and your annuitant dies. Your account is worth $200,000 but the enhanced death benefit (high water mark) locked in at $300,000 and is payable to you! Sure, taxes would be owed on the gain but you received your losses. You receive $300,000 with only the $200,000 gain being taxable. This is a way to take a very calculated approach to managing risk with specific assets. A thirty year old can take a portion of their riskiest asset class and position that asset in such a manner calculating that someone 45 years their senior is probably going to pre-decease them and make this work. The objection here is that if the thirty year old dies before the 76 year old then The $200,000 (current value and not the enhanced death benefit) is payable to the contingent beneficiary. Knowing there were a contingent beneficiary named, because someone doing this type of planning would understand that not having named a contingent beneficiary the annuity proceeds to go to the owners estate and end up in possible probate court-not *advisable!. Annuities are generally not a probate asset unless foolishly planned or mistakes are made in the structuring. It is always advisable to have contingent beneficiaries.*

Chapter II

The Contract Owner

In this chapter we will discuss the contract owner: specifically, the owner's rights, duration of ownership, taxation, death, joint ownership, and effects of IRS rules on the owner. Most of the rights to the benefits associated with the annuity belong to the owner.

NON-NATURAL OWNERS
IRC Section 72(u)

The owner is not required to be a natural person. A non-natural entity (such as a trust or corporation) can be the owner of an annuity. However, unless an exception exists, non-natural owners lose tax deferral on income accumulated in the contract. In addition, "income on the contract" would be taxed annually as earned whether the income were distributed or not.

Ownership of an annuity by a (CRT) Charitable Remainder Trust does not retain the tax-deferred status. (PLR 9009047) However, keep in mind that a CRT itself is tax exempt, and its income is taxable only upon distribution under CRT tax rules. Section 72(u) of the Internal Revenue Code governs the rules associated with non-natural owners. As you will see these rules have exceptions:

RULE #1:

Contributions made to contracts after February 28, 1986 would have the non-natural rule apply. However, there is no IRS guidance regarding the tax treatment of income on contributions made prior to this date. Many tax advisors recommend not commingling contributions. Making further contributions to contracts that have "grandfathered" contributions would not be the best approach nor advisable.

RULE #2:

To determine what constitutes "income on the contract", you may follow this formula: (net surrender value + all distributions received) MINUS (total net premiums + all amounts previously taxed).

For Example:

In 1999, a Corporation purchases a $100,000 non-qualified deferred annuity on the life of its president. December 31, 1999, the net surrender value is $110,000. The Corporation must include the $10,000 gain in the contract as ordinary income on its 1999 taxes.

In 2000, the Corporation contributes $100,000 to the contract. On December 31, 2000 the net surrender value is $210,000. The Corporation has no taxable income to report that year.

December 31, 2001, the Corporation has a net surrender value of $250,000 AFTER the Corporation withdrew $50,000 earlier that year. The Corporation would have ordinary income of $90,000 in the year 2001. Taxes would be due on the $90,000 ($50,000 gains withdrawn + $40,000 gains remaining in contract from the previous year).

In 2002, the Corporation does not withdraw or add money. However, the net surrender value has grown from $250,000 to $310,000. The Corporation would owe ordinary income tax on the $60,000 gain within the contract.

EXCEPTION #1

The "AGENT" exception rule allows tax deferral if the annuity is owned by the non-natural entity, and holds the annuity as "agent for a natural person".

For Example:

Tax deferral would not be lost if the Corporation holds a group annuity for its employees (each of whom has a certificate for their participation).

EXCEPTION #2

The "minor (child) owner" is technically the legal and beneficial owner even if a guardian is named as owner (FBO) for the benefit of the minor. Tax deferral should not be lost. The same holds true for (UGMA) Uniform Gifts to Minors Act accounts.

EXCEPTION #3

(Grantor Trusts) There have been numerous IRS private letter rulings (PLR) indicating tax deferral would not be lost, if an annuity is owned by a trust, all of which is treated for income tax purposes as owned by a natural person. *(PLRs do not bind the IRS to cases outside the PLR and do not make or change tax code. Each PLR is valid for that specific case only. However, these PLRs show the likely IRS position on such cases. See PLR 9322011, 9316018, 9120024).* Grantor Trusts will be considered held as agent for a natural person under the "grantor trust" rules of IRC Sections 671-679. Grantor Trusts are commonly referred to as revocable trusts as well. However, certain circumstances exist where irrevocable trusts can qualify for tax deferral as well.

EXCEPTION #4

Immediate annuities do not have the non-natural person rule. However, the annuity must be single premium and payments must begin no later than one year from the date of purchase and must provide for substantially equal periodic payments (at least annually).

EXCEPTION #5

If the death of the owner causes the annuity to become part of an estate the non-natural person rule does not apply.

EXCEPTION #6

An annuity that is held under a "qualified" plan, IRA, 403b, TSA (tax sheltered annuity), etc. would not be subject to the non-natural person rule.

EXCEPTION #7

A so-called "qualified funding asset" used in a structured settlement is not subject to the non-natural person rule.

EXCEPTION #8

If an annuity is purchased by an employer upon termination of a qualified plan and held by the employer until all amounts are distributed to the employee or the employee's beneficiary, the annuity would not be subject to the non-natural person rule.

OWNER'S RIGHTS

The contract owner has certain rights under the contract. While the annuitant is alive, the owner generally has the power to do the following:

- Allocate Sub-account Funds within variable annuities
- Transfer funds within different sub-accounts
- State and change the annuity starting date
- Name the annuitant (changing is not an absolute right)
- Choose (and change, prior to the annuity starting date) the payout option

- Request and receive the proceeds of a partial or full surrender
- Amend the contract with the issuing company's consent (annuities are a bi-lateral contract-both parties must agree to any amendments)
- Assign or transfer ownership of the contract to other parties
- Initiate and change systematic withdrawals

The owner can name the annuitant, but may not be able to change the annuitant. Some annuity contracts specifically state the owner's right to change the annuitant and some do not. This is not a universal right as those mentioned above. For instance, if the owner of the annuity contract is not a natural person (a trust), a change of the annuitant is treated the same as if the owner has died for income tax reasons. This means certain distributions must be made from the contract due to IRS regulations. So, even if the contract allows the owner to change the annuitant, special care should be taken in naming the annuitant when the owner is not a natural person. This will help to avoid possible negative tax consequences. Remember, the non-natural rules typically look to the annuitant when following distribution rules.

CESSATION OF OWNERS'S RIGHTS

If you notice in the above list you will see the clause "while the annuitant is alive". Under MOST annuities, the owner's rights in the contract cease when the annuitant dies. Then, one of two things happens: either the value* of the contract is paid to the beneficiary or the beneficiary becomes the new owner. The only way for a beneficiary to become the new owner is for an exception to be made under the Internal Revenue Code Section 72(s). This exception is known as Spousal Continuation. Under the Spousal Continuation exception the primary beneficiary must be the spouse of the contract owner, and the contract owner must be deceased or have been changed. There cannot be more than one primary beneficiary and it must be the spouse! You can name contingent beneficiaries. If the owner dies in either an "owner driven" or "annuitant driven" policy, spousal continuation can be claimed if the spouse is named as sole primary beneficiary. Yet, if the annuitant in an "annuitant driven" contract dies, spousal continuation does NOT apply! An easy rule to remember is, "deceased owner's spouse may continue the contract, if named the sole primary beneficiary."

This does not present a problem when the owner and the annuitant are the same person. However, care should be taken when naming an annuitant. Before I show you an example you must understand all annuities must have a stated annuity start date. This is the date at which the contract should commence annuitization or distributions should begin.

For example:

Larry has a deferred annuity and the maximum age in which the annuity starting date may be deferred is age 80. However, Larry turns age 81, and he wants to take income through systematic withdrawal rather than annuitization. In order to maintain the annuity in its deferral period, Larry names his son Philip, age 45, as the annuitant. Larry retains ownership of the contract so he can take systematic withdrawals. It is also very important to know beforehand if the company will send the owner or the annuitant the income. Some companies will allow the owner to choose.

Larry's rights would cease in the event of Philip's death and Larry would lose control of his funds. To avoid this risk Larry could also name himself as beneficiary under the contract. Under this arrangement, Larry would incur income taxes on the earnings if the annuity value were paid to him upon Philip's death. However, Larry got the proceeds, not another party. Philip could be named a contingent beneficiary in the event of Larry's death. The illustration below illustrates the scenario.

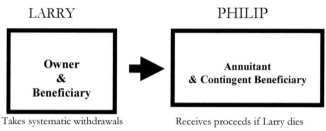

Under some contracts, the owner's rights do not cease automatically when the annuitant dies. If the owner is not the annuitant, and the annuitant dies first, some contracts provide that the owner automatically becomes the annuitant. Other contracts provide for time to allow the owner to choose another annuitant if a contingent annuitant was not named. After a period of time, if no annuitant is renamed, the owner will become the annuitant.

Sometimes people may want another party to own their annuity for estate planning or tax reasons. If a purchaser names a trust as owner, certain forms of trust ownership may shift income and estate taxation of the benefits of the contract away from the purchaser. However, the purchaser may be liable for gift taxes on the value

The Truth about Variable Annuities

of the annuity and/or the premiums paid on it. By giving up ownership of the contract, the purchaser also gives up all contractual rights to control the annuity. A purchaser could name a trust the owner and still retain control over the trust, but such a trust would not shift the income or estate tax liability away from the purchaser. Proper tax or legal counsel should be sought with regard to trusts.

OWNER'S TAXATION

Generally speaking, the owner of an annuity is the entity that is taxed on any "taxable amounts distributed" from an annuity during the annuitant's lifetime. This is true even if someone other than the owner is receiving the annuity benefit payments. Remember, an owner can be a natural person or non-natural entity. If the owner were a non-natural entity, that entity would not have tax deferral of any gains in the contract. Any gains would be taxed annually at the entity's ordinary income tax rate. *Again, naming another person to receive the payments does not shift the tax liability away from the owner.* Only a gift or other transfer of ownership can do that with consequences. However, some contracts make the annuitant the owner when a contract is annuitized. Also, with certain exceptions, if the owner of the annuity is not a natural person, the annuity does not provide income tax deferral or accumulations. Major exceptions to the nonnatural person rule (IRC section 72(u)) are a trust acting as agent for a natural person, a qualified plan, or the estate of a deceased owner. (See Chapter 2 for more information on Trusts (IRC Section 72(u)).

Section 72(s) of the IRC tells us about the required distributions regarding the death of the owner of an annuity contract. Federal tax law requires that certain distributions be made from the annuity in the event that ANY owner dies. If the contract owner is not a natural person, the annuitant will be looked at and treated as the owner for death distributions and tax purposes. (Trusts)

If an owner dies:

- AFTER THE ANNUITY START DATE: assuming owner is not also the annuitant, any remaining payments under the annuity must be made at least as quickly as the payments were being made prior to the death of the owner.

- BEFORE THE ANNUITY START DATE: the entire value of the annuity must be distributed within 5 years of the date of the owner's death, or the value of the annuity must be annuitized within one year of the date of the owner's death payable to the listed beneficiaries.

SPOUSAL EXCEPTION

The SPOUSAL EXCEPTION rule is easy to remember if you can remember these three words, "Deceased Owner's Spouse". These three words will help you remember spousal continuation. The deceased owner's spouse may continue an annuity contract, only if the spouse is named as the sole primary beneficiary. No other primary beneficiaries can be named. Contingent beneficiaries can still be named. One "Teflon Coat" that can be applied with divorce in mind, is naming the primary beneficiary as "current spouse of the contract owner upon owner's death". This would allow for a divorce and the new spouse is automatically the primary beneficiary without doing anything. This allows for no legal misinterpretations as the word current could have been arguably to mean current was at the time the policy was written and not the "current spouse" upon death. There are many ways to write this but care should be taken and mostly thought about from the defending point of view. Always think how an heir or mad ex-spouse would want to twist the word in their favor. Thinking this way would help in forming the right language.

The Truth about Variable Annuities

JOINT OWNERSHIP

Joint owners can be either natural people or non-natural entities. Rules are designed to prevent the use of joint-ownership to obtain tax deferral on annuity earnings over more than one person's lifetime, except for married couples. The required distribution rules apply to contracts issued after January 18, 1985. Joint ownership today by married people can be desirable. Having husband and wife as joint owners and naming "the surviving spouse" as primary beneficiary allows for spousal continuation. Remember, you may want to clarify "surviving spouse". What was meant by that statement? Was it current or former spouse? Who is to clarify spouse, the courts?

EXAMPLE 1

Larry and Kelly jointly own an annuity with a cash value of $100,000 and an enhanced death benefit of $200,000. The primary beneficiary is named "surviving spouse". Upon the death of Larry OR Kelly the survivor is allowed to receive the $200,000 death benefit from the insurance company while at the same time allowing the survivor to continue the contract without any taxation until the proceeds are taken out of the annuity as long as the beneficiary designation reflects the spousal continuation rule (surviving owner/spouse)!

EXAMPLE 2

Another example: Larry buys a deferred annuity with an initial value of $100,000. Larry names himself the owner and himself the primary beneficiary on his "annuitant driven" contract. He makes his grandmother (age 75 and in bad health) the annuitant. The annuity start date of his contract is age 90 for the annuitant. He feels his grandmother will be deceased prior to age 90 due to her health. He wants this structure because it allows him to be in the market with his variable annuity with a death benefit guarantee. If his $100,000 grows to $200,000 and the death benefit value locks in at $200,000 he knows he has protected his gains if it went down from there! If his grandmother dies he will receive a minimum of $200,000, as he is primary beneficiary of his own annuity. The tax ramifications would be the income tax owed on the gain in the contract. He put in $100,000 and received $200,000. The $100,000 gain would be taxed at ordinary income tax levels.

Now, let's get back to joint ownership. I wanted to tantalize you with some "structure strategy" and how to benefit from using structure. A jointly owned annuity is not like a joint bank account. Do not confuse the two. With a joint annuity both owners' signatures are required to exercise rights of ownership. In addition, if a withdrawal were taken, both owners would receive a 1099 form. Each would get a 1099 for half the amount of the withdrawal. Each joint owner would be held liable for the tax consequences. Any joint owner under age 59 ½ would also be liable for the 10% IRS penalty on the gains within the contract, unless an exception applied. You cannot have joint ownership in IRA's!! This is prohibited of the current tax law. *However, having written this book over several years I can now attest that one company is seriously pushing the rule boundaries and will allow joint owners in an IRA. Think about it from a common sense* standpoint. IRA stands for <u>INDIVIDUAL RETIREMENT ACCOUNT</u>. If I contribute to my IRA I get to write-off the contribution from my AGI up to the limit of the max IRS deduction. Therefore, what does the joint owner get? Do they get any write-offs? Do we (together) get to double the amount we can contribute and write-off? Can we co-mingle our IRA assets in this manner? I can tell you it is definitely not worth the risk to litigate with the IRS when your retirement income is at stake and you may end up with lots of money wasted on litigation and less income than needed. Also, this company that allows this touts a PLR (I will not name it or the PLR). However, PLR stands for Private (one) Letter Rulings and typically apply to one contract and not an entire company product line. Unless a tax ruling or IRS exemption that has been clearly attained in writing and is made to a company and they will provide this document to you, I would stay far away from this type of set up. This is the stuff that causes companies to lose good ratings and potential nightmarishly long and costly litigation. I would feel sorry for the shareholders that bought the insurance company stock when this litigation hits!

If a party becomes the joint owner of an existing deferred annuity, that new owner has the same rights and privileges as the existing owner. In addition, the original owner has now made a taxable gift to the new joint owner unless they are married (unlimited marital deduction). The original owner would be income taxed on the gains up to half the value since the new owner would now own 50%. A possible gift tax may also apply beyond the current free gift limit, and possible 10% IRS penalty of gains if the original owner was under age 59 ½ at the time of the gift. Just adding a joint owner has serious consequences if the new joint owner is not a spouse!

DIVORCE

Let's discuss divorce and annuities. If you get divorced and have an option to give the deferred non-qualified annuity or the house (that has equity), give the annuity! A QDRO (Qualified Domestic Relief Order) issued by the judge in the divorce would allow the annuity to be given to the former spouse. Some tax authorities have claimed the spouse receiving the annuity must pay all the income tax, gift tax, and 10% penalty if under age 59 ½ rather than the gifting spouse due to the QDRO. The QDRO shifts the tax burden to the receiving spouse. A divorce decree is different. Some tax authority's state there is no taxable consequence due to the QDRO. I will not provide any comment on this as I for do not know since even the IRS has provided me with conflicting details a nd advice. Again, everything is subjective until ruled upon.

In addition, under the QDRO the spouse that keeps the house with equity in it can keep up to $250,000 tax-free under current tax law when the house is sold! In a divorce decree, neither spouse would owe the taxes until the annuity is distributed. Then, the current owner would be taxed and/or penalized. This illustration assumes current tax laws.

Chapter III

The Annuitant

What exactly is an annuitant? Many contracts define the annuitant as the individual who is designated to receive the income benefits under the contract and/or upon whose age the payments are based. Under some contracts, as well as in the tax law, the annuitant is defined as the individual upon whose life "income payments" will be based; the benefits themselves may be paid to another party. If this is the case, the annuitant still remains the "measuring life" in reference to those benefits. The annuitant must be a natural person(s). If a trust or corporation were named as the annuitant, there would be no natural life to measure the benefits of the contract. The role of the annuitant is similar to the insured in a life insurance policy. An annuitant's age is the primary factor that determines the benefits. The attainment of a certain age of the annuitant triggers the annuity starting date. In many cases the annuitant is the owner as well. This is the simplest structure form and one of the most common. Being the most common does not make it the best, by any stretch of the imagination! However, we will discuss other favorable structures later on.

ANNUITANT RIGHTS AND TAXATION

An annuitant has few rights under the contract. The most important is the right of the annuitant to receive annuitized income payments. However, if the company allows, the annuitant may direct (assign) the payments to a third party. The annuitant would remain the taxable party if annuitization has commenced, even if a third party were receiving the payments! However, if any other form of distributions were paid to a third party, the contract owner would remain the taxable entity. Annuitization is the primary form of distribution that triggers the change of taxable entity, from the contract owner to the annuitant. This is very important to understand in the new age of living/income benefit riders on variable annuities.

JOINT ANNUITANTS

Contracts can have a single annuitant or joint-annuitants. They can also have contingent annuitants already named in case of death of the annuitant. There is increased risk of unwanted changes if more than one annuitant is named and death occurs to an annuitant in a deferred non-qualified annuity prior to the annuity start date. This is due to the risk of death for either of two people is higher than the risk of death for one person. If one of the annuitants dies, some contracts pay the value of the annuity to the beneficiary immediately. Some contracts allow the remaining joint annuitant to become the sole measuring life of the contract. Others may allow the contract owner to change the annuitant designation. However, if the owner is not a natural person (Trust), this change of annuitant would cause a mandatory death benefit payment distribution to the designated primary beneficiary and taxes would be owed. If the company would allow the remaining annuitant to be the measuring life it would be best for continued tax deferral.

<u>Under an "annuitant driven" contract, upon the death of the annuitant, the proceeds (proceeds in this example should be the enhanced death benefit) will be paid immediately to the primary beneficiary.</u> Remember, some companies (in an annuitant driven contract) will not pay a death benefit until the remaining joint annuitant dies or the IRS forces the death distribution due to the Owner dying. Knowing if a company pays a death benefit upon the first or second annuitant's death is a main factor in planning with "annuitant-driven" contracts. There is no need to name joint annuitants to get a desired "joint and survivor" guaranteed annuitized lifetime income stream.

TAXATION AND ANNUITANTS

I mentioned earlier that the tax consequences of the annuity are the owner's responsibility. Upon annuitization the annuitant becomes the taxable party. Some company's also force a change of ownership to the annuitant upon annuitization so the tax consequences flow properly to the person receiving the income. There is an "exclusion ratio" that applies to annuitized contracts and must be included to calculate tax consequences. For non-qualified (non-IRA) annuities, there is a return of principle when annuitization commences. Each payment would have a tax-free portion for the return of principle and a taxable portion.

DEATH AND ANNUITANTS

Death of the annuitant, as mentioned earlier, can have major or no changes to a contract depending on the contract language. Remember under "annuitant-driven" contracts the proceeds would be paid to the beneficiary. Under an "owner-driven" contract the owner could decide the new annuitant if there was no named contingent annuitant, the owner could become the annuitant or the co-annuitant will become the sole annuitant. If an annuitant dies AFTER the annuity starting date the payments would continue under the terms of the payout to the newly named annuitant. In many cases if death of the annuitant occurs after the annuity start date the owner automatically becomes the annuitant. The annuitant is the simplest to understand of the 3 parties involved in an annuity.

CHANGING ANNUITANTS

There is no right granted to changing the annuitant. Some contracts specifically grant the owner the right to change the annuitant and some do not. Remember, that if the owner of the contract is a non-natural person, a change of annuitant would be treated the same as the death of an owner for income tax purposes, which means certain distributions may be required.

Chapter IV

The Beneficiary

This chapter will focus on the beneficiary. I will discuss and explain the following:

- What is a beneficiary?
- Multiple beneficiaries
- Minor beneficiaries
- Taxation and beneficiary
- Beneficiary Death
- Non-natural beneficiaries
- Beneficiary changes-revocable and irrevocable
- Contingent beneficiary
- Disclaimed assets by a beneficiary.

WHAT IS A BENEFICIARY?

The beneficiary of a contract is the entity that would receive the proceeds of an annuity contract upon death of the owner OR annuitant or owner AND annuitant. Notice I said "entity", and not person. A trust, corporation, or business can be the entity that receives these proceeds. Unlike the annuitant, there is no requirement that the beneficiary be a natural person. While the "benefits" of an annuity flow primarily to the owner or the annuitant, the beneficiary is only sort of a "remainder man" designated to receive the proceeds upon death of one or both of the remaining interested parties (owner or annuitant).

MULTIPLE BENEFICIARIES

There can be more than one named beneficiary. Generally, the owner would specify the beneficiary(s). Named beneficiaries can receive differing amounts or percentages at the owner's discretion but if not noted most companies would split the proceeds equally. In addition, if multiple beneficiaries were named and the death benefit was annuitized then the oldest named beneficiary's age is used for annuitization purposes.

MINOR (Child) BENEFICIARY

Naming a child a beneficiary can cause problems. Many states and insurance companies have differing views on what age constitutes a minor. Generally, to be safe any person under age 21 should be considered a minor. If a beneficiary must be named and has not attained the age of 21, the contract's owner should have a will and name a guardian to receive the benefits on the child's behalf. The guardian should be clearly named on the contract. Otherwise, there could be a delay in benefits until a court appoints a guardian. One way to name the guardian of a minor child beneficiary is to state the following as the designated beneficiary: "John Smith, Guardian—(FBO) For the Benefit of Sally Smith".

TAXATION AND BENEFICIARY

When a beneficiary receives the benefits from an annuity, he or she becomes liable for income taxes on the gain within the contract. A beneficiary can also be liable for the 10% IRS penalty tax on premature distributions, due to the language in the tax law regarding the definition of "pre-mature distribution" for non-qualified annuities. The language in the tax law refers to the taxpayer's age. Upon death of the owner or annuitant, the proceeds are payable to the beneficiary. Rather than becoming the owner, the beneficiary can become the taxpayer. I will further detail beneficiary taxation with illustrations in later chapters since there are many different structures available that can affect taxes due by the beneficiary.

A beneficiary has four (4) options available upon receiving annuity proceeds. He or she has the option to take the proceeds in a lump sum. Second, the beneficiary may defer income for up to five (5) years, and then must liquidate the annuity. Third, the beneficiary may commence annuitization over their life expectancy and/or term period. And finally, if the sole primary beneficiary is the surviving spouse of the deceased owner, they may elect to continue the annuity in their name.

BENEFICIARY DEATH

Death of a beneficiary prior to the owner or annuitant's death could result in benefits being paid to the dead beneficiary's estate. Naming a contingent beneficiary would eliminate that outcome. If a beneficiary dies prior to the owner or annuitant the owner can name a new beneficiary.

NON-NATURAL BENEFICIARY

A non-natural beneficiary would be considered an entity other than a person. A non-natural beneficiary has two (2) of the possible four (4) distribution options available. The non-natural beneficiary could take a lump sum or defer distribution of the proceeds for up to five years. In any case, if distribution is required due to the death of the owner or annuitant, distribution of the full amount must be made within five (5) years.

BENEFICIARY CHANGES

The owner has the right to change the "revocable" beneficiary at any time without notice to the named beneficiary. When a beneficiary has been named as an "irrevocable beneficiary" on the contract, the owner must seek permission from that beneficiary and notify the company in writing in order to change or add a beneficiary. Generally the owner and irrevocable beneficiary will sign the forms necessary for a change to occur. Unless specifically noted as "irrevocable" the beneficiary would be considered revocable.

CONTINGENT BENEFICIARY

The owner can name a contingent beneficiary on a contract. Although it is not required, it is a good idea. If a beneficiary dies prior to the owner or annuitant, the contingent beneficiary would become the beneficiary of record. As with multiple beneficiaries, there can also be multiple contingent beneficiaries on a contract. Contingent beneficiaries need not be a natural person either.

DISCLAIMING by BENEFICIARY

The beneficiary can disclaim the assets they are entitled to prior to receiving those assets. Why would someone purposely disclaim an asset? Sometimes it is a necessity when a contract has beneficiaries improperly named. For instance, in regards to his estate planning, dad wants upon his death, his annuity proceeds to go only to his children that are named contingent beneficiaries. However, his wife is named as primary beneficiary. His wife could disclaim the assets and allow the flow-through of assets to the contingent beneficiaries (kids). If a beneficiary (wife) disclaimed the assets and there were no other named beneficiary (primary or contingent) then the proceeds would revert back to the estate of the owner (dad). Thus, forcing the annuity (which is generally a "non-probate" asset) to possibly become an asset likely sent to probate court.

Revocable & Irrevocable

An owner may name an irrevocable beneficiary but once named the beneficiary must consent to allow the owner to make changes in the future that may dilute their future inheritance.

Chapter V

DEATH BENEFITS

It is very important to understand your death benefit. You should know when your death benefits stops growing or locking in. You should also know if upon a certain age if you have not died you may lose your death benefit. You should understand how other features and benefits may affect your death benefit or possible even eliminate it altogether.

All annuities have a standard death benefit. The original money (all premiums) deposited within an annuity is the underlying minimum guaranteed standard death benefit. However, many annuities today offer a variety of death benefits. Offered by the insurance company as an additional "rider" to the contract, these enhanced death benefits act as additional insurance or guarantees. Enhanced death benefits and estate planning death benefits generally cost the investor more. These death benefits can be calculated in a variety of ways. The death benefit is most important with regard to the structure of the annuity contract. The contract will specifically state which death benefit is payable upon the death of a certain party to the contract (annuitant, owner or both). We will explore these variations individually in this chapter.

Standard Death Benefits

Generally, all annuities offer the standard death benefit of the original amount of premium deposited, unless the contract specifically states a different amount or calculation. *If you opened an annuity with $100,000, the death benefit would immediately be $100,000. There is generally no cost for the standard death benefit, considering the mortality and expense charge for the annuity usually have this actuarially factored into the cost.* Generally, the standard death benefit is paid regardless of which party dies (owner or annuitant).

Enhanced Death Benefits

Enhanced death benefits usually cost the investor additional .10% to .70% basis points annually. That would translate into $100.00 per $100,000.00 to $700.00 per $100,000.00 annually. Enhanced death benefits can be calculated in a variety of ways. It is very important to understand when an enhanced death benefit is payable. Upon a certain party dying (annuitant or owner) the enhanced death benefit would be paid. If the annuitant dies in an Owner Driven contract the standard death benefit may apply. However, if the Owner dies in an Owner Driven contract the enhanced death benefit would apply. In later chapters the illustrations of annuity structure will explain this in more detail.

A common method of calculation is the annual contract anniversary date. Every year the contract would have a new death benefit guarantee on the anniversary. Some contracts allow a certain percentage growth factor known as "annual step up". Many variable annuities or indexed annuities offer "high water marks".

STEP UP DEATH BENEFIT

In the step up death benefit, the annual anniversary is usually the date in which the insurance company would guarantee your initial deposit by a certain percentage. If a contract guaranteed a 5% step up, and the original deposit were $100,000, upon the first annual anniversary, the death benefit would be $105,000. The following annual anniversary would then take the $105,000 and multiply the 5% to it. This would allow the compounding of the death benefit as well. It is extremely rare to find a step up death benefit that is calculated using simple interest rather than compounding interest.

HIGH WATERMARK/Lock-in

While it is most common for annuities to calculate the high water mark on the annual anniversary, some allow daily, monthly or quarterly watermarks. An example would be for an investor with a deposit of $100,000 on July 10th, 2005 invests in a variable annuity. On the annual anniversary (July 10, 2006) the account value reached $125,000. This would be "locked in" as the new death benefit. However, on July 10, 2007 the account value dropped to $113,000. Most contracts allow the $125,000 to remain the enhanced death benefit. Some contracts allow only the last years locked in amount ($113,000). For those contracts that allow for "quarterly or monthly" watermarks the calculation would be the specified time period within the contract.

It is very important to understand the death benefit within the annuity contract. The step up or high watermark death benefit usually stops at age 80 or other specified time. Some contracts revert back to the cash value at the end of the guarantee period. So, at age 80 if the owner has a cash value of $200,000 with an enhanced death benefit of $250,000, the new death benefit may be cash value ($200,000) from age 80 and beyond. Many contracts today will lock in and NOT revert to cash value unless the actual cash value is higher than the "locked in" death benefit!

Chapter VI

LIVING BENEFITS

A living benefit is obviously the opposite of the death benefit. A contract holder does not have to die to benefit from a living benefit. However, a triggering event would allow the living benefit to be payable. Living benefits usually cost the investor additional .10% to .70% basis points annually. That would translate into $100.00 per $100,000.00 to $700.00 per $100,000.00 annually.

Living Benefits are generally calculated by on the step up or high watermark values, similar to the way death benefits are calculated. Most true "Living Benefits" must be annuitized. A "withdrawal Benefit is different in that annuitization is not required or allowed. This chapter will focus primarily on Living Benefits. The benefits would be calculated, and then payments would be made from a specified calculation. Living benefits are benefits that will be provided while the specified contract party is alive. Generally there is a 5-10 year holding period to enact the living benefit under the annuitization clause. But in most cases there is the ability to derive income immediately while protecting your annuitization living benefit for future use.

Living benefits can be payable to the owner or annuitant. Generally the tax liability stays with the person receiving income. Sometimes, upon utilizing the annuitized living benefits of a contract, the ownership will shift to the annuitant. The annuitant is whose life the payments are based off and who will generally receive payments.

LIVING BENEFIT STEP UP

A living benefit that allows a step up, as mentioned earlier in the death benefit chapter, would allow for annuitized payments to be made. For instance, if the owner of an annuity has a 5% guaranteed living benefit, the contract would step up (compound) annually at that amount for a specified time period (usually age 80). A $100,000 contract would be worth $105,000 after the first year. A $100,000 contract after 10 years would be worth approximately $162,889. If the variable annuity cash value were only $140,000 due to bad market performance, the owner could annuitize the $162,889 living benefit. If a 40 year old held a $100,000 annuity with a 5% living benefit until age 80, the guaranteed living benefit, which could be annuitized, would be ($100,000 compounded at 5% for 40years) approximately $703,998.87. That means an investor age 40, could have invested in the variable annuity and the market for 40 years and still be guaranteed the $703,998.39 regardless of his market value at age 80. He could annuitize the $703,998.39 if his cash were much lower! We have not even talked about the high watermark yet!

There are numerous annuitization options available. Most annuitization options allow for payments to continue to the beneficiaries for a specified amount of time upon the death of the original payable party (annuitant). This allows for the investor's heirs to make sure they receive what is owed them, unless a "Life Only" option is chosen. "Life Only" allows only the payable party to receive the living benefit payments and upon their death the payments would cease. Obviously, this is not a popular option. There is also the ability to take the payments over two lives. Husband and wife could opt for a joint and survivor payment from the living benefit. The 5 most common living benefit payment options are:

1. Life Only
2. Life 10
3. Life 15
4. Life 20
5. Joint Life 20

For example, Life 10 allows for payments to be made for a minimum of 10 years or for the entire life of the payable party (annuitant). If the payable party (annuitant) dies 5 years into the payments, the payments would continue to the heirs for another 5 years. The highest payment is for the Life Only option. The lowest payments are for the Joint Life options.

HIGH WATER MARK

The high watermarks are generally calculated on an annual basis via the contract anniversary. It is possible for a living benefit to allow for a high watermark that is calculated daily, monthly or quarterly. I have seen contracts that allow high watermarks to be calculated more often than "annual anniversary".

The following example will allow for both living and death benefits to be illustrated from a step up and annual anniversary calculation:

John purchases an annuity with $100,000 on June 15, 2005. The contract allows for a 5% (living and death benefit) step up and annual high watermark. On June 15, 2007 the value reached $300,000. On June 15, 2015 the value was $200,000. John has held the contract for 10 years.

On June 15, 2015, John has a death benefit and living benefit of $300,000 (high watermark). He also has a step up death and living benefit of approximately $163,000 (step up at 5% annually for 10 years). Since the $300,000 high watermark is higher than the step up

($163,000), the $300,000 is the guarantee of the living and death benefits for this example. If John dies his beneficiary would receive the $300,000 death benefit. Since John is alive, he could take the $300,000 living benefit and annuitize it. (Some companies make the earliest annuitization at year 10.)

Chapter VII

Pro-Rata vs. Dollar for Dollar

Funny Math….

It is of utmost importance to understand how withdrawals from an annuity contract affect the contract guarantees. There are many ways in which a contract holder can take income from an annuity. Regardless of age, IRS penalties, (RMD) Required Minimum Distributions, systematic withdrawals or withdrawals outside of annuitization. Withdrawals play a very important role in annuities. Remember, all annuities have the "standard" death benefit with options of additional enhanced death benefit and living/income benefit "riders". All withdrawals outside of annuitization will affect these contract death/living guarantees.

An annuity will generally have a provision for taking withdrawals and will explain how those withdrawals will affect the contract guarantees. The withdrawal methods that affect the annuity contract are known as either Pro-Rata or Dollar for Dollar. To understand Pro-Rata or Dollar for Dollar distributions you must fully understand the guarantees associated with living and death benefits. Understanding what makes one method better than the other is based on which withdrawal method maintains the contract guarantees in differing markets, and what affect it has on the amount of income (withdrawals) available.

With regard to Variable Annuities, different markets known as a "Bear Market" (Decreasing) or a Bull Market (Increasing) in conjunction with withdrawals, can have inverse affects on a variable annuity where Pro-Rata or Dollar for Dollar distributions are concerned. Pro-rata distributions are typically similar to "dollar for dollar" distributions in variable annuity contracts when the account is rising in a "Bull Market". The primary reasons Pro-Rata withdrawals may be better than Dollar for Dollar, is that Pro-Rata may allow for increased income while maintaining the same benefits that Dollar for Dollar offers. In contrast,

Pro-Rata withdrawals will provide less income than Dollar for Dollar while maintaining the same benefits in a "Bear Market" (decreasing). So, knowing which calculation is used by your annuity company should be of concern when purchasing an income benefit. Your income and the volatility/fluctuation of that income can depend on the market swings and how the calculations are made.

While it may be easy to choose which variable annuity should be used for income in a Bull or Bear Market, predicting both the market and when an investor will need income causes the most concerns with annuity planning. The case for diversification holds true in this case as well. Having annuity contracts that affect withdrawals on both a Dollar for Dollar and Pro-Rata basis will eliminate the problem of predicting the markets when income is needed. Let's take a closer look at a few examples of withdrawals and how they affect the benefits in both a Bull and Bear Market. What will be illustrated is any form of distributions or withdrawals, but not annuitization. The stated benefit used in the above example could be a death or living benefit, or both. The main point here is in knowing if the calculation of any benefit is pro-rata or dollar for dollar.

BULL MARKET Example:

An annuity offers a 5% compounded guarantee (stepped up Living benefit or death benefit- it does not matter.) John is age 60 and invests $100,000 in an annuity. This means John would have $105,000 "Benefit Guarantee" at the end of the first year. John wanted some monthly income and decided to start taking his 5% (Living Benefit) annually. He has been receiving his monthly income; however, John's account still grew to $150,000 at the end of the first year.

In the Dollar for Dollar contract he may only take 5% ($5,000) annually, of his "Original" premium ($100,000) to maintain the original $100,000 benefit. His actual cash value at the end of the year was $150,000 and locked in and now became his new benefit level. However, many companies only allow the 5% income to be taken off the original premium amount ($100,000). This means that John can continue taking his $5,000 yearly income on a monthly basis but his account is now locked in at $150,000. One way to overcome this and increase John's income is to take approximately 4.77% of the $150,000 and it will allow for the benefit level to remain the same but allows john more income (4.77% of $150,000 = $7,155.00). Still less than the pro-rata calculation but still more than $5,000! Beware of this as some companies do not allow the 4.77% calculation off the high water mark!

In the Pro-Rata contract John may take 5% of the "actual cash value" ($150,000) and not the original premium! John would now be able to take $7,500 in income and maintain the same $100k /$150k benefit (living or death). His actual cash value after the withdrawal will be $142,500 ($150,000 - $7,500). <u>John would be able to take more income in a Bull Market from a Pro-Rata contract while maintaining the original guarantees.</u>

BEAR MARKET

In the same example, an annuity offers a 5% compounded guarantee. (Living benefit or death benefit- it does not matter.) John is age 60 and invests $100,000 in an annuity. This means John would have $105,000 "Guarantee" at the end of the first year if no income was taken. However, John's account lost money and at the end of the first year the actual account value was $80,000. John decided to take a withdrawal (income) at the end of the first year. He took his 5%.

In the Dollar for Dollar contract he may only take 5% ($5,000) of his "Original" premium ($100,000) to maintain the original $100,000 benefit. His actual cash value was $80,000 prior to the $5,000 withdrawal and his benefit level was $105,000. After the withdrawal of $5,000 his account cash value would be $75,000 with a $100,000 "benefit" guarantee (living benefit or death benefit). This is where the term "dollar for dollar" comes from. His actual amount of withdrawal ($5,000) reduced his cash value and the benefit level by the actual amount taken! Something to consider as a smart investor is, the $5,000 withdrawal represents a 6.25% withdrawal (income) from the actual cash value ($5,000 / $80,000 = 6.25%). The $5,000 withdrawal represents a 5% withdrawal from the "original premium" ($100,000 X 5% = $5,000). Taking a 6.25% withdrawal from your investments to live off is worrisome as it represents a higher than average income from a portfolio. At this rate you may go broke fairly quickly! But with the dollar for dollar benefit rider you would be able to do this for several years until your cash is minimized and then annuitize under the benefit rider or take income for life under the benefit. You would not have any "cash value" to get your hands on in an emergency but you would have income! Remember that once the contract has been annuitized under the rider or regular annuitization there is no death benefit. Any remaining benefit that would be paid to a beneficiary would be that based on the annuitization benefits chosen.

  In the Pro-Rata contract John may take 5% of the benefit level and the contract in this example performs similar to a dollar for dollar contract.

  It all comes down to how the annuity company calculates the withdrawal and from what number it is calculated. In Dollar for Dollar, the 5% withdrawal is taken based off the "ORIGINAL PREMIUM" in order to maintain the original guarantee. In Pro-Rata, the 5% withdrawal is based off the original guarantee or the newest step up/lock-in value in order to maintain the original guarantee.

In the next chapter you will learn about exchanges and replacements. However, I need to address something VERY IMPORTANT in this section as well since we are addressing dollar for dollar vs. pro-rata for you to understand the significant differences in the examples provided. Imagine you have $10 in your right pocket and $100 in your left pocket. You want to buy a $2 Coke, so you use the $10. Your change is $8. If I told you that your Coke purchase has affected the spending power of the $100 in your left pocket by the same proportion would you understand what I mean? Let me explain: you spent 20% of the $10 ($2). So, you must now reduce the $100 by the same percentage (20%). That means you now only have $80 in your left pocket. You are probably catching on by now and figuring the $2 Coke really cost you $20. That is the very foundation of pro-rata. The right pocket that contained the $10 is your cash in your annuity contract and the $100 in your left pocket is the benefit of your annuity contract riders. If your contract has lost value (represented by the $10) and you started taking income (spending money to buy a Coke) it would reduce your annuity rider benefits by the same percentage. Dollar for dollar would have reduced the $100 by the same actual cost of the Coke, $2. So, with dollar for dollar you would have $8 in your right pocket (cash) and $98 in your left pocket (benefit). As you can imagine it is becoming harder and harder to find contracts that offer dollar for dollar benefits. Most new contracts today that offer dollar for dollar, usually only offer it up to the percentage of benefit offered (5%, 6% or 7% maybe 10%). Let me explain. If a contract offers a dollar for dollar benefit of 5%, you could withdraw up to 5% and it would affect the benefit by the actual cash taken (dollar for dollar). Imagine you have $100k *cash value* and your *benefit* is $200k. You can take 5% of the $200k ($10,000) as income and it would reduce your cash by $10,000. That $10,000 actually represents a 10% withdrawal of your cash value but a 5% withdrawal of your benefit value. All is well. However, if you exceeded the 5% and needed to take say $20,000 that year you have violated the contract. That extra $10,000 would reduce your cash by the total amount you withdrew ($20k-your cash is ALWAYS reduced on a dollar for dollar basis but the benefit is not) but your benefit would be dealt with differently. Your first $10k (5% of the $200k benefit) is calculated on a dollar for dollar basis but the next $10,000 would be a pro-rata calculation. So, your cash value was $90,000 after the approved 5% withdrawal and now you took another $10,000 of the $90,000 cash value representing an 11.11% extra withdrawal. Now your $200,000 benefit must be reduced by the same percentage of 11.11%.

That extra $10,000 would now cost you $22,220 and your new benefit level would be $177,780. This would affect your next year's income as you could only contractually receive 5% of the $177,780 ($8,889) on a dollar for dollar basis, anything excess withdrawals beyond this would have the same former negative affects to the contract! That one extra $10,000 withdrawal has now forever affected your income and reduced it from $10,000 annually to $8,889.

IMPORTANT!!

Some older contracts state the entire contract is dollar for dollar for any and all withdrawals. If you took that extra $10,000 out of one of those contracts you would not have this negative impact!! Knowing which contract you have is of extreme importance! To better provide you with how experts would plan using this knowledge please read the next few pages, including my "Author's Note" and the very first "Great Example"!!!! This will illustrate a full vs. first 5% dollar for dollar benefit. Now, ask yourself if you own an older contract that has vast benefits that are no longer offered? Ask yourself why the media, attorneys and talk show hosts encourage you to get rid of that bad annuity. By taking their prudent advice you may have already given up hundreds of thousands of dollars of potential future income benefits! If an advisor encouraged you to swap (replace or exchange) an annuity for a newer one did they perform the proper due diligence in finding out what type of contract you have? Did they fully understand all the ramifications of the swap? If so, they may have been able to provide you EXTRA BENEFITS! This is all shown in the next example after Author's Note! Read on…

Chapter VIII

AUTHORS NOTE:

Careful consideration should be taken if MORE income is needed during a Bear Market. The account could be depleted faster since more income would be taken in addition to the Bear Market losses. Many prudent Financial Planners feel Pro-Rata is a better contract in both markets. These planners feel it forces the clients to realize the potential of going broke faster by taking an increased "percentage" of income based on actual cash value, in addition to the losses of a Bear Market. Pro-Rata allows for *increased income in Bull Markets with less potential of going broke due to a lower "percentage" of income based on actual cash value, with additional gains. A simple prudent rule to follow is, "income derived as a percentage of actual cash value should remain the same in any market". (For example, take a 5% income annually from your <u>account balance</u> and not the benefit balance in any market!) This would allow the underlying funds to last longer rather than taking income as a dollar amount in any market or percentage of original premium. (For example, if you started with $100,000 portfolio and took a 5% income of that original* *premium, and the account has had a 50% loss in a Bear Market, your $5,000 income the next year would now be translated into a 10% income as a percentage of "actual cash value" of $50,000.) It makes even more sense when you take a look at market history. In any market environment, taking a 5% income stream from actual cash value versus a 10% income stream will obviously allow for the income to last longer!*

A great example

Imagine you are age 60 and have a non qualified contract you opened with $100,000. Over some time period it grew to $500,000 and now it is worth $300,000 in cash value. If you cash it in you get $300,000 with $200,000 being taxable at income tax rates. However you could take advantage of the living/income benefit of $500,000 and take income for life. Having a FULL dollar for dollar benefit annuity you can have the best of both! You could take almost all the cash value ($299,000) out pay your taxes on the $199,000 gained in the contract. This leaves the contract cash value of $1,000. It would reduce your living/income/death benefit by the same amount of the withdrawal ($299,000). But the $299,000 reduced the $500,000 benefit now worth $201,000. So, you have $299,000 in cash (minus taxes) and can take advantage of the living income benefit of $201,000. This would provide you income for life based off $201,000 benefit and you also have 99% of cash value ($299k) too!

If you tried this in a pro-rata contract you would get the same cash but you would have depleted your income benefit! The reduction would not be the same as the withdrawal. Since you took $299k from $300k that represented a 99.66% withdrawal and your $500,000 income/death benefit would be reduced by that same percentage! So you would have $1,000 cash value left in the annuity contract with a living/death benefit of roughly $1,700 that would be used to take 5% income for life! ($85.00 per year!) Yeah, that equates to a few dollars per month! Before you give up your current annuity or take income or money out to buy that car, you better know which type you have!!!

Now, here's what an expert would do in this situation: perform a partial 1035 exchange so no taxes would be due immediately. That would leave your old annuity with $1,000 in cash value (right pocket) and $201,000 in benefit (left pocket). The new contract would have $299k in cash and benefit. Now, here is what gets interesting. Imagine you did nothing. You still have your old contract. Your $100k grew to $500k went down to $300k and today it is back up in value to the $500k. You would have $500k cash and $500k benefit- remember these numbers! All is well, right? NO! By performing the partial 1035 exchange and the same performance occurred you would have increased your income and benefits. Let me explain! Remember the old contract now has $1,000 with a $201k benefit. The new contract has $299k in cash and benefit. You still have the same cash just in two separate contracts. By moving the $299 cash into a new contract it allows for new step ups if the market grows rather than in the old contract it would be making up loses that are already insured by the benefit. If the same growth occurred that would have meant the $299k in the new contract grew by $201k. That growth would have locked in providing you a new benefit of $500k and $500k cash value. Now add this to the old contract cash value and benefit and your calculation should show $501,000 cash value and $701,000 benefit value between both contracts. This contract has $500k benefit and the old still has $201k benefits. This contract has $500,000 cash value and the old one has $1,000. <u>If you had done nothing, your old contract with a value of $300k would have grown back to the $500 just like the</u>

second contract with $299k did! Your old contract's gain wiped out the benefit that you have been paying for all along!! So, replacing an annuity is not bad as everyone wants you to believe! In many cases there is more liability in doing nothing! Now, that I have explained the truth about replacing annuities we can discuss compliance and exchanges, better known as the "Sales Reluctance Department!" Many firms frown upon exchanging annuities and make it almost impossible for advisors to perform. Their fear of losing their clients benefits, causing financial lose of benefits, potential litigation and not having the willingness, time or knowledge to make sure such replacements are proper makes for them to seem to be the bad guys. Their fear is well founded as these products are complicated and there are hundreds of companies and thousands of annuities in the marketplace, each with different moving contractual parts. Do not blame them; they are doing their best to protect everyone from harm. If your advisor is an expert he/she should be very able to navigate the complexities of their compliance department in most cases. Sometimes those twenty-something's in compliance are not knowledgeable enough and won't allow the replacement simply out of innocent ignorance.

You must also remember that annuities are so complex and they must be sold, not bought. Many investors call their broker to buy a hot stock. In all my years I have never heard of an investor calling up their advisor demanding to buy an annuity. This "selling" is what causes everyone to harp on annuities. Make no mistake "selling" takes place everywhere…. "Would you like to supersize that?"

Chapter IX

Compliance and Exchanges

The regulatory environment today has made switching from one annuity to another very complicated in regards to making sure the switch is beneficial to the client. This may seem elementary; however, as you have seen there are many very complicated issues that must be taken into consideration prior to a switch. The form at the end of this chapter will help shed light or at least make the benefits and pitfalls of switching more noticeable.

There are numerous reasons people want to switch from one annuity to another. The new annuities (1997 and newer) have vast benefits that older annuities do not. These are known as Living Benefits, Enhanced Death Benefits, Withdrawal Benefits, and Estate Planning Death Benefits.

Older annuities typically came only with the standard death benefit or a multi year step up (after 7 years the death benefit would lock in on the 7th anniversary.) Today almost all annuities offer an annual lock-in on the anniversary. Typically any other feature or rider added to the base annuity cost the investor additional fees. This may be where the media and other investment competitors (like mutual funds) want to point the finger about higher costs associated with the annuity. Never have I seen where the media or investment competition does a fair and unbiased job of explaining the benefits of the higher cost. What is intriguing is the proven fact that the underlying investment funds not only cost significantly less in the annuity than the retail mutual funds but have in many cases outperformed the retail mutual funds. The outperformance may come from the fund manager having the ability to sell a position for profit and not having to worry about the capital gain distribution to the fund since the fund assets for the annuity are held inside a V.I.T (Variable

Insurance Trusts) and is part of the annuity and not the retail fund where the capital gain distribution has affects (taxes)! In addition, the numerous studies have shown where the actual cost of ownership of the same fund is almost double in the mutual fund versus the variable annuity when all elements of the two investments are compared.

Taxes seem to never play a role and yet are the most important factor in the determination of true cost of ownership when funds and annuities are compared. When investors see the vast benefits derived from annuities, they tend to purchase the annuity. In addition, they are always on the lookout for a new annuity that may better suit their needs, calling for a switch or more appropriately, a "replacement".

QUALIFIED CONTRACTS

Before discussing replacements we must first understand there are two types of contracts:

Qualified and Non-Qualified. Qualified contracts are those in which qualify as a retirement account under section 401(a) of the IRS code. These can be IRA, SEP, 403b, 401k or any money that has been contributed by the individual prior to taxes taken out (tax deferred). When money is moved from one account (replaced) in a qualified account it is known as a "transfer" or "trustee to trustee transfer".

NON-QUALIFIED CONTRACTS

A Non-Qualified contract is a contract that has after tax money contributed to it. When these accounts are replaced they are known as a "1035 exchange". The IRS code 1035 is the section of the code that permits such movement of money on a non-taxable basis, hence the "exchange". When an annuity is exchanged for another annuity there is no tax consequence if it qualifies under section 1035. Many people are familiar with the 1031 exchange in Real Estate. These are non-taxable exchanges for differing assets within the same class and must qualify under their respective codes.

It is always best to have some form of a due diligence process in which to evaluate a replacement of an annuity. The problem of late is there is no program in place. Advisors choose what makes for a proper replacement or worse yet; have their back office choose what constitutes a proper replacement, typically by broad guidance. In reality, back offices tend to lay down blanket rules regarding replacements that make little or no sense other than some compliance attorney knows someone who knows someone that got sued in a weird way and their replacement rules were made in reaction to that lawsuit. I will never understand why Broker Dealers do not have their own expert to compile a set of replacement rules that can coexist for the benefit of the clients and the reduce liability of the firm. Rather, they seem to just join the media and say all replacements are bad. As you have seen in numerous examples, replacements can not only be good, but there may be serious retained liability for NOT REPLACING just as there is liability in replacing! What needs to be done is a true analysis of the client for all annuities, new and replacements.

Example #1: A Good Replacement

Tim, age 86, has a net worth of $2 million. He has a non-qualified annuity worth $500,000 and plans on leaving that to his heirs or at least use this money as a last resort if he goes broke in his other money. At 86 he knows there is not an annuity in the world that allows for a death benefit other than his original $500,000 premium. He purchases an annuity without a CDSC (no surrender charge). He has full liquidity and can access all the money at any time without any company imposed fees or penalties for that access. This type of contract is commonly known as a "C" share annuity (there are also "no-load" annuities available). He bought the annuity on June 10, 2005 with $500,000. On July 28, 2006 his annuity value is $600,000.

Here is the key to a proper replacement!!!

If Tim's annuity value goes back down to $550,000 and he dies his heirs would get the cash value of $550,000. However, if Tim were to replace the annuity when it reached $600,000 and 1035 exchange it for an identical type (no-load or "C" share) the <u>new annuity</u> would guarantee the beneficiaries the $600,000 purchase premium. So, when the account went down to $550,000, using the same example, the $600,000 standard guaranteed death benefit would be paid to his beneficiaries by his <u>new annuity</u> if Tim were to die and the account had gone down to $550,000.

Example #2: A Good Replacement

Blake has an existing annuity that offers a living and death benefit on a dollar for dollar basis in regards to withdrawals. Blake opened the annuity with $100,000 non-qualified assets (after tax money). His living and death benefit is now worth $300,000 and the current cash value is worth only $200,000. Blake could perform a partial 1035 exchange on $199,000 to a new annuity. This would allow $1,000 to remain in the old contract with a living and death benefit of $101,000!!!! Remember, on dollar for dollar contracts you simply subtract the amount from the cash value and benefit guarantees. This leaves a contract that has little cash value but high living benefits. Blake did not lose his living or death benefit in this replacement. In fact, to <u>not</u> replace this annuity at this point should be malpractice! <u>Why? Because if the $200,000 cash value were long term money and remained invested in the market and grows back to the $300,000 and the replacement did not occur, Blake would have a contract that has a cash value of $300,000 and benefits of $300,000.</u> The re-gain in the contract relieved the insurance company of their risk (rider benefit) that Blake was paying for!!

If he performed a partial 1035 and the new $199,000 grew back to the $300,000 he would have the old contract worth $1,000 in cash value and $101,000 in benefits and the new contract worth $300k in cash and $300k in benefits. This totals between two contracts $301,000 in cash value and $401,000 in benefits!!

Old contract $300,000 benefit		$200,000 cash value
-$199,000		-$199,000 1035 exchanged
$101,000 benefit		$1,000 cash value
New contract $199,000 benefit		$199,000 cash value
+$201,000 growth		+$201,000 growth
$300,000 benefit		$300,000 cash value

Add the old contract and new contract to get total value.

Old	$101,000 benefit	$1,000 cash value
New	$300,000 benefit	$300,000 cash value
Total	$401,000 benefits	$301,000 cash value

As you can see there are numerous reasons for replacements to occur and I advise you not to take to heart what you hear in the media regarding annuity replacements.

Following is a worksheet to help identify whether a replacement is in the best interest of the investor. Take the old annuity and fill in the blanks on the left side of the sheet. Fill in the form with the information from the proposed new annuity.

Then, compare each line item to one another. Place a green check mark to the item that makes more sense or fits the investor more appropriately. Place a red "X" on the one that does not fit or is inferior. Add up the green checks and red "X's" on the left and right sides. The one with more checks wins- so far! Now you must take a closer look at the red "X's" on each. If an "X" is on an item in the old annuity the investor may want to watch out more closely on those "X" items over the short term. If the new annuity won, the red "X's" should be paid very close attention to. These red "X's" could cause the potential problems. This will ensure the annuity owner fully understands the good, bad, and ugly of either retaining the old annuity or the new annuity. In a worst case scenario it allows for a great starting point for a review!

Chapter X

Annuity Replacement Worksheet

DATE_____ CLIENT&AGE_____ ADVISOR_____

EXISTING ANNUITY

Issue Date_____ Policy #_____
Company/Rating_____
Contract Name_____
M & E _____ + admin _____ = _____
Owner-driven_____ annuitant driven_____
Owner_____ Joint_____
Annuitant_____ Joint_____
Beneficiary_____
Original Deposit $_____ Date_____ Basis $_____
Current Cash Value $_____ Date_____
Surrender Value $_____ CDSC_____ %
Remaining CDSC Schedule_____ %
CDSC Waivers_____
Death Benefit $_____ 4 or Pro-rata
DB Cost ____ % Compounded @ ____ to age ____
High water mark_____ to age_____
Spousal Continuation_____ Restricted_____
Living Benefit $_____ 4 or Pro-rata
LB Cost ____ % Compounded @ ____ to age ____
High water mark_____ to age_____
Annuitization schedules_____
Withdrawal Benefit %_____ cost_____ %
Free Withdrawal amount %_____
Withdrawals after annuitization yes____ no____
Money Mgrs_____ # Sub Accounts_____
Performance_____
Fixed account %_____ MVA_____
**Company Pre-emptive Language?

_____
_____

Risk Tolerance_____ Risk_____
Client Signature_____ Date_____

PROPOSED ANNUITY

Transfer Amount $_____ Bonus_____
Company/Rating_____
Contract Name_____
M & E _____ + admin _____ = _____
Owner-driven_____ annuitant driven_____
Owner_____ Joint_____
Annuitant_____ Joint_____
Beneficiary_____
Basis $_____
Current Cash Value $_____ Date_____
CDSC Schedule_____
CDSC Waivers_____
Death Benefit $_____ 4 or Pro-rata
DB Cost ____ % Compounded @ ____ to age ____
High water mark_____ to age_____
Spousal Continuation_____ Restricted_____
Living Benefit $_____ 4 or Pro-rata
LB Cost ____ % Compounded @ ____ to age ____
High water mark_____ to age_____
Annuitization schedules_____
Withdrawal Benefit %_____ cost_____ %
Free Withdrawal amount %_____
Withdrawals after annuitization yes____ no____
Money Mgrs_____ # Sub Accounts_____
Performance_____
Fixed account %_____ MVA_____
**Company Pre-emptive Language?

_____
_____

Risk Tolerance_____ Prosposed_____
Client Signature_____ Date_____

The Truth about Variable Annuities

Chapter XI

The Truth about Step-Ups

Daily vs. Monthly vs. Quarterly vs. Annually

Perception is not reality most of the time. Many times our human brain takes something we think is true and makes us feel confident in things we do not fully understand because we rationalize it or familiarize it. Think about it for one moment, if you could lock in your gains at the highest point of each DAY vs. each YEAR common sense tells us that daily lock-ins are better, right? The math even works; 240 times a year when the market is open you have a chance to lock in a new high whereas you get only once per year (your annuity contract anniversary) on the annual lock in. Now, here is the truth that nobody wants to discuss. There is no free lunch-ever. First, there is a risk premium that must be paid for this benefit well beyond the premium paid for an annual lock in. This higher cost is oftentimes poised as a higher benefit; if it cost more it is better. Good marketing ploy but not spot on.

An example here is your home. You may feel it is worth $200,000 but it is really only worth what some willing buyer (with the money) will pay for it. Say what you want, you cannot argue with the real answer above. Same goes for the daily vs. annual step up feature.

I figured it would be easier to discern the two benefits that are farthest apart to provide a larger disparity for the example. What nobody wants to talk about are the rules that must be followed with the purchase of a daily, weekly, or quarterly step ups. In many cases, since the insurance companies have increased risk they must mitigate that risk somehow. First they charge more and second they lessen the market risk they must insure. Many advisors and clients think they get the highest daily lock in of the stock market. They actually receive the lock-ins based on their portfolio after many rules and calculations are followed. Many annuities have caps or restraints that mute the potential growth. Higher fees will stifle the return as well. The most common way companies mitigate the risk to these benefits is to force a specific allocation. This allocation must be very well diversified and may force a larger portion to a fixed or cash (low risk) bucket that could have the effect of watering down the return.

In some instances, the advisor and client allow the actual fox that is watching the chickens to make the decisions. What I mean is the insurance company has the right to go into your account and reallocate your portfolio and put up to ALL your money into a fixed account that is earning between almost nothing (.25% - 3%.) They will typically perform this reallocation after a significant loss has been had in the market that previous day. So, after you have lost money they now take it out of the market and place it in a fixed account. An example; if you have $100,000 and today your portfolio suffers a 2% market correction (-$2,000). The insurance companies may go into your account and reallocate a very large portion (say 15% or $15,000) to the fixed account that pays up to 3% per YEAR. This allows that $15,000 to earn a guaranteed rate of return of 3% per year ($450) and it would remain there in the fixed account until the $2,000 loss was made up. That is over 4 years that 15% of your money is not getting market returns or the daily step up but your fees for the benefit are continuing to be charged on the entire account! Wow, all this for one little bad day in the market? Well, remember there is no free lunch and smart actuaries at these insurance companies have figured out one thing; mitigate the risk but keep the product sexy so it can be sold! Keep it complicated and many advisors will swear by it when approached by another company's representative trying to educate them and show them these issues while trying to pitch their own product and compete. This is where the breakdown occurs. Advisors and clients feel they fully understand these benefits; after all daily beats annual right?

Let's discuss annual lock-ins to get a clearer viewpoint as well. An annual step up generally costs much less but locks in on the contract anniversary once per year. Most do not reallocate to any fixed account and some do force at least some diversification. Diversification is not a bad thing. However, I will provide significant examples of strategies that can be utilized later.

Overall, if you plan on keeping an annuity for long term income/death benefits these guarantees should probably be only a few dollars to a few hundred dollars apart per monthly income benefit when you need to depend on the income guarantee. However, the cost would have been many thousands of dollars apart, the longer the time the more the disparity of cost. In many cases the maximum amount a company will guarantee (called caps) is reached before the annuity holder utilizes the annuity benefits. They could be stuck in an annuity that will not grow any more from a benefit level for years. They would keep it since their cash value is so far below the benefit level and is unlikely to surpass the benefit level (annuity jail). If they cancel the annuity and buy another one they would lose the benefit as one company would not honor another company's benefit level. With proper planning you can choose the right annuity. Otherwise you end up with little differences, as almost all would eventually provide the same benefit as any other annuity if not properly sold. The daily lock in may cap out faster so if your income need is sooner this may be right for you. But know that the others will catch up to them eventually and may even grow more since they are un-capped with lower fees! You will see these at a finer detail when I provide strategy examples later.

Chapter XII

The Strategies

DISCLAIMER: *The following are to be considered only examples of ways you can manipulate and utilize variable annuities to some extent. Not all examples may be available today and may not provide the intended consequences due to tax law or company changes to product features. The following is meant to engage and open your mind to the many different options of using a variable annuity. Mostly, I want to show how they may have been used in the past by experienced advisors, intelligent investors and the greatest wholesalers. Lastly, I want to help you understand the benefits and truth about variable annuities and how they can possibly be structured to provide "extreme" benefits. Just like a basketball in Michael Jordan's hands can be very different than in the hands of a first grader. Maybe this will illustrate how an annuity sold by experts can be something much more!*

1. *Extreme Benefits with Diversification*

I want you to imagine that you are about to buy a variable annuity with $400,000. It is a great annuity provided by a great company with a knowledgeable advisor. If I could show you that by using the exact same annuity, same advisor, same insurance company, same costs, and same benefits and by simply knowing how the benefits work and properly structuring your annuity that you will receive 25% more value after one year, would you believe me? No worries. I will prove it to you now so that you know the truth.

<u>The scenario</u>: *a 5% living/death benefit with a highest anniversary locks in.*

If you buy one annuity with the $400,000 and for simplicity you diversify your money equally into 4 assets classes; Growth, Growth and Income, Technology, Bonds. Let's assume that upon the first contract anniversary your account value remains $400,000 but your guarantee is the highest value that day or at least 5% on the $400,000. You get your annual statement and it shows your cash value is $400,000 your guarantee is $420,000 ($400k times 5%). There was not highest value lock in on the total account since the market was flat.

However, looking back at the historical changes in that first year you noticed something. The portfolios were acting wildly. (For this example I will show extreme things that have never happened in my experience but I want to make a point of how to benefit from this strategy.) Your portfolio fluctuated wildly and in the end it looked like this:

- Your Growth Fund ($100k) ended up doubling and finished at $200k
- Your Growth/Income Fund ($100k) fluctuated but ended back at its beginning point of $100k
- Your Technology Fund allocation ($100k) went bust and went to zero-now $0
- Your Bond Fund allocation was stable with no increase/decrease and remained at $100k

Now, let's do simple math and see where your account value lies. Growth $200k + Growth/Income $100k + Technology $0 + Bonds $100k = $400,000 cash value. The account has a guarantee of 5% or highest total account value, so your guaranteed living/death benefit would be 420,000. ($400k times 5%) That is the typical benefit and the average advisor would tout how great it performed in such a crazy market. You leave the annual review with your advisor, happy that you did not lose money and even happier you have a guarantee. WAIT! There was a better way!

Now, imagine you bought four SEPARATE annuities from the same advisor / company / benefits -everything the same. You just bought four. You only have $400,000 so you bought four separate $100,000 annuities. You allocated them exactly the same;

- **Annuity #1**---100% allocated to the Growth Fund-$100k
- **Annuity #2**---100% allocated to the Growth/income Fund-$100k
- **Annuity #3**---100% allocated to Technology Fund-$100k
- **Annuity #4**---100% allocated to Bond Fund-$100k

In order to avoid the aggregation rule of the IRS it has been suggested that you name different owners/annuitants for each. The aggregation rule pertains to the amount of assets includable as taxable income upon annuitization and first in fist out rules etc. It is too complex to fully illustrate here—just know you need to make material changes.

- *Annuity #1* Husband owner-Wife Annuitant
- *Annuity #2* Husband and Wife Owners Husband Annuitant
- *Annuity #3* Wife Owner and Husband and Wife Joint Annuitants
- *Annuity #4* Wife Owner and Husband Annuitant

One very simple way to avoid the aggregation rule is not purchase more than one annuity from the same insurance company in a calendar year. If you do, the example above shows you a potential means of avoiding the aggregation rule. Having multiple insurance companies' guarantees not only diversifies your benefits but also your company risk (if an insurance company fails). Most are covered by State guarantees and other means so don't worry but it saves you from having all your money tied up and dealing with regulators of a failing insurance company!

Now let's look at why you may have used this strategy using 4 different annuities! Remember the benefit is based on the entire annuity and not each allocation in the first example using only one annuity. Having Annuity #1 allocated to Growth with the same amount $100,000 has its own guarantee of 5% or highest value. Knowing it is worth $200,000 on the anniversary locks in that $200,000! Annuity #2 remained at $100,000 cash value but has a guarantee of $105,000. Annuity #3 cash value is zero but is worth $105,000 in guarantee! Annuity #4 remained at $100,000 cash value with a guarantee of $105,000. Now, let's add:

- Cash value of all the annuities combined is $200k + $100k + zero + $100k = $400,000 total cash value. (Same value as example using only one annuity contract)
- Benefit Value of all the annuities combined is $200k, + $105k + $105k + $105k = $515k in benefits. ($515k vs. the one annuity of $420k)

Now let's compare the one annuity strategy:

- Cash Value of the one annuity is the same $400k due to Technology wiping out the Growth Funds gains)
- Benefit Value is $420,000 not $515,000

So, there is a $95,000 difference in the benefits using the exact same, EVERTHING. Knowing how these benefits work and what to do allows for great planning and while using every benefit offered! Having an advisor with significant knowledge of contract structuring and IRS laws allows for even more in-depth planning! You could avoid the aggregation rule and properly structuring the annuities may alleviate multiple future issues (divorce, death, etc) as well as potentially providing for more financial benefits even more by using dollar for dollar contracts! This would allow for much more liquidity in this case. (See the pro-rata vs. dollar for dollar example at the end of that chapter)

2. Too age-challenged (old) for a benefit?

The Truth about Variable Annuities

Old is a very relevant term. My children think I am old as dirt at 39. I am sure those over age 75 think the same way. It all depends on your outlook and how you feel! But for the moment, imagine you are age 75+, a very fee conscious investor or advisor and need/want to remain invested in the market with a portion of your assets. Since most insurance companies start to reduce or eliminate their benefits at age 75 I used this as a starting point for this example. This strategy is an idea to reallocate that stock market money/position (riskiest asset). Take that asset and position it inside a variable annuity if it is already exposed to that level of risk. Many variable annuities do not offer a death benefit at the older ages. There is one way to get a free one though!

Ask your advisor to sell you a "C share" or no load variable annuity. Invest your asset in it and diversify up to the same risk tolerance you were before. This does not expose you to any more risk and in many cases may actually lower your actual fees/costs! Many management accounts (wrap fee programs or SMA's cost over 2%). Most of the C Share annuities cost about 1.5% plus fund fees .50%-1% making the cost difference minimal! A no load annuity would reduce your total costs under 1.5%! That includes paying your advisor too! Remember all annuities must provide a non-forfeiture provision and a corridor of death benefit to be considered an annuity. There are other determining factors, but let's keep it simple.

Why would you do this? As stated all annuities come with an "original premium/deposit" death benefit at no cost! That means your $100,000 that is exposed to the same risk before you allocated to the annuity can go down as well but be protected for your heirs. If the stock position went to $50,000 and you died the heirs get $50,000. In the annuity if the same occurs and the annuity is worth $50,000 the death benefit is $100,000-the original deposit (less withdrawals—pro-rata or maybe dollar for dollar—know your contract!!!!) If the contract went up to $150,000 you should ask your advisor to perform a 1035 exchange and buy another companies annuity. Why? Because when you move the $150,000 to another company that company takes the $150,000 in as a new deposit/premium and the full $150,000 is now protected whereas if you stayed in the current annuity and the market went to $150,000 and back to $50,000 your heirs only get the $100,000!

3. Bringing me more Alpha!

To keep this simple and not bring too much industry jargon into the equation; when someone talks about "alpha" it simple means increasing a return without increasing the risk. It can also mean lowering the risk but retaining the same return. It pretty much involves risk and has to do with amounts of risk taken. The goal of financial planning is capital appreciation, capital preservation or income. What if we were to discuss all of these and achieve all of these together? Think about your allocation to the lowest and highest risk class of your allocation currently. Say, money market (cash) and emerging market stocks. These two allocations (low/high risk) are always part of a good financial plan. You need them to be properly diversified. However, the amount in which you allocate will determine the risk taken. More allocated to cash equals a more conservative portfolio.

What if you were able to raise the return of your cash like investments and guarantee those wide swings and high points of your riskiest asset class? Would that appeal to you? I would never suggest compromising your liquidity needs but consider your low risk and low return assets when I say "cash" or money market. Placing these assets into a variable annuity with living/death benefits allows for the guarantee of income or death benefit to heirs that your current allocation cannot provide while allowing you to maybe take more risk to gain more return in your low risk asset. Maybe your low risk asset provides a 3% return. The annuity may allow a 5% income guarantee or higher if the market locks in on the income guarantee! The high risk asset has not lock-ins and could double or go bust. You have seen earlier in example one how high flying goes bust and you still benefit! This is something to think about when allocating specific money to annuities. I am not sure if it makes sense to take a well managed greatly diversified portfolio and put into the annuity unless I knew more of the details of the investor. What are you trying to accomplish? Think of your money in buckets of income and risk. This will allow you to think more openly about what should go into an annuity if any at all.

It is important to understand that I use the 5% amount as an example and many contracts offer 7% and some up to 10% guarantees!!

NOTICE:

ILLUSTRATING THE ANNUITY STRUCTURE

The following illustrations attempts to simplify some of the numerous structures that are possible, so as to help further your understanding of structuring the annuity contract. I have also decided to show market fluctuations. Every example will be based on <u>non-qualified</u> (non-IRA) <u>VARIABLE annuities prior to the annuity starting date unless specified.</u> The <u>amount deposited</u> will be <u>$100,000</u> and will <u>grow to $500,000</u> at the highest point (locked in for death and/or living benefits), then <u>drop back to $300,000</u>, which reflects <u>the current market value and time of death or distribution.</u> This will help define and explain amounts that are taxable and paid to certain parties with differing structures. No withdrawals will be illustrated unless noted. Dollar for Dollar or Pro-Rata distributions are not illustrated unless withdrawals are illustrated.

Remember, there are hundreds of Insurance Companies; thousands of different annuity contracts, and each could have State differences. This entire book as well as these illustrations are for example only, and intended to help you understand the possible outcomes, and are not to be construed as absolute fact or law. Consult your financial advisor, tax advisor and/or legal counsel for guidance. These illustrations have been compiled from sources that are considered very reliable; however, they should only be considered expressions of the author's opinion. The author cannot guarantee the complete accuracy due to changing tax laws, differing contracts, insurance company rapid changes, and State law differences.

Structuring Examples

EXAMPLE #1
*Owner Driven Contract

OWNER/ANNUITANT   BENEFICIARY
Husband   Wife

DEATH of Husband:

     Wife has 4 options:
1) She can take a lump sum $500k
2) Defer distributions up to 5 yrs (some companies will allow for equal distributions over the 5 years with taxes due upon each distribution)
3) Annuitize $500k within one year
4) Continue the contract in her name and name new beneficiary (Beware- some companies would force continuation of the contract at the $300k cash level whereas some companies would actually add $200k to the contract and allow for wife to continue the contract with $500k and some will also allow for and surrender charges to waived).

Federal Income Tax:
1) Distribution under the first three options would be taxable to wife at ordinary income tax rates on the gain ($400k)
2) Option #4 would allow the Federal Income Tax to continue to be deferred

Federal Estate Tax:

1) Wife is U.S citizen; value of contract is includable in husband's gross estate for marital deduction.

Federal Gift Tax: None

Death of Wife: A new beneficiary should be named but the contract remains intact in husband's name. There are no Federal Taxes due.

*ANNUITANT DRIVEN Contract:

Everything remains the same even if this contract were an ANNUITANT DRIVEN CONTRACT (Using the same example) since the death of the husband equated to the death of the owner & annuitant (enhanced death benefit would be paid in either situation of owner or annuitant driven contracts). Spousal exception rule would also apply (spousal continuation would be granted since wife is the spouse of the deceased owner and named a sole primary beneficiary.

EXAMPLE #2
Owner Driven Contract

OWNER	ANNUITANT	BENEFICIARY
Husband	Wife	Husband/Wife

DEATH of Husband:
    Wife has 4 options:
1) She can take a lump sum $500k
2) Defer distributions up to 5 yrs (some companies will allow for equal distributions over the 5 years with taxes due upon each distribution)
3) Annuitize $500k within one year
4) Continue the contract in her name and name new beneficiary (Beware-some companies would force continuation of the contract at the $300k cash level whereas some companies would actually add $200k to the contract and allow for wife to continue the contract with $500k and some will also allow for and surrender charges to waived).

    Federal Income Tax:
1) Distribution under the first three options would be taxable to wife at ordinary income tax rates on the gain ($400k)
2) Option #4 would allow the Federal Income Tax to continue to be deferred

Federal Estate Tax:

1) Wife is U.S citizen; value of contract is includable in husband's gross estate for marital deduction.

Federal Gift Tax: None

Death of Wife: A new beneficiary should be named but the contract remains intact in husband's name. There are no Federal Taxes due.

Here comes your first curveball—I will illustrate this same example with an "Annuitant driven" contract and notice the amounts that would be paid to beneficiary!! (There is a $200k difference!)

*Annuitant Driven Contract

DEATH of Husband:

Wife has 4 options:
1) She can take a lump sum $300k (this was annuitant driven therefore the enhanced death benefit payable is only the cash value not the death benefit!
2) Defer distributions ($300k)up to 5 yrs (some companies will allow for equal distributions over the 5 years with taxes due upon each distribution)
3) Annuitize $300k within one year
4) Continue the $300k contract in her name and name new beneficiary. Her death benefit should remain the same at the $500k level and name a new beneficiary. . Most companies would not waive any surrender charges

(CDSC) for this death (husbands) since there was not death a benefit payable.

Federal Income Tax:
1) Distribution under the first three options would be taxable to wife at ordinary income tax rates on the gain ($400k)
2) Option #4 would allow the Federal Income Tax to continue to be deferred

Federal Estate Tax:
1) Wife is U.S citizen; value of contract is includable in husband's gross estate for marital deduction.

Federal Gift Tax: None

DEATH of Wife:
Husband only has 3 of the 4 options: *Husband cannot continue the contract since he is not the "spouse of a deceased owner" according to IRS regulations (section 72s). He is the owner and remains alive.* HUSABAND CAN:
1) Take lump sum of $500k and pay ordinary income taxes on gain
2) Defer $500k distribution for 5 years then pay ordinary income taxes on total gain
3) Annuitize $500 within one year.

Federal Income Tax:

1) All deferred income taxes payable at ordinary rates when distributed to and received by husband. *If the husband is under 59 ½ years old he may also have to pay the excise tax (premature distribution penalty under IRC section 72q) of 10% of all gains in the contract.*

Federal Estate/Gift Taxes: NONE

EXAMPLE #3
*Owner Driven Contract

OWNER	ANNUITANT	BENEFICIARY
Husband & Wife	*Husband*	*Surviving Joint Owner*

DEATH of Husband or Wife:
    Survivor options:
1) Take a lump sum of $500k
2) Defer distribution up to 5 yrs
3) Annuitize $500k within a year
4) Continue the contract and become the owner and the annuitant and name anew beneficiary.

(Beware-some company's contracts do not pay out the $500k until the last owner's death and some will not waive CDSC charges and may also force continuation at the lower cash value level ($300k). It would be important to know if the enhanced death benefit is payable upon the first owner or second owners death if there are joint owners of a contract.)

Federal Income Tax:
1) If the contract is continued the taxes remain deferred otherwise ordinary income taxes are payable by the survivor beneficiary as distributions are received.

Federal Estate Tax:
1) Half of the ($300k or the $500k depending on the contract) would be includable in the gross estate of the first to die but it would qualify for the marital deduction if the surviving spouse were a US citizen.

The Truth about Variable Annuities

Federal Gift Tax: None

CURVEBALL:

Same example but now *** Annuitant Driven**!

Death of Husband: *would be the exact same as Death of Husband or Wife just illustrated.*

Death of Wife (much different-loss of $200k!)
Husband's Options:
1) Lump sum of only cash value $300k (*since the enhanced death benefit is payable only upon the death of the "annuitant in an annuitant driven contract!*)
2) Defer the distribution of the $300k up to five years
3) Annuitize the $300k within one year
4) *Continue the contract with $300k cash value and $500k death benefit and become the owner and annuitant as well as name a new beneficiary.

Federal Income Tax:
1) If husband continues the contract taxes remain deferred but when income is distributed ordinary income taxes would be due.

Federal Estate Taxes:
1) Half of the $300k would be includable in the gross estate of the wife but the marital deduction would apply assuming the husband is a US citizen.

Federal Gift Tax: None

The Truth about Variable Annuities

EXAMPLE #4
*Owner Driven Contract-

Owner	Annuitant	Beneficiary
*Non-Natural Entity *(Revocable Trust)	Husband	Wife

Death of Husband would trigger the death benefit as the Annuitant would be the "measuring life" to pay a death benefit. However, some "Owner-Driven" contracts may not pay out the enhanced death benefit ($500k) since the owner was a non-natural entity and therefore could not die so they would pay out the $300k. Some contracts would not look through the non-natural entity to the annuitant in order to pay out the enhanced death benefit. This is very important to know before purchasing the annuity if a non-natural entity was to be named the owner. In many cases this occurs with estate planning scenarios and the repercussions are not known or felt until it is too late. This is usually the beginning of litigation for all parties involved!

The Federal Estate tax consequences would make the value ($300k or $500k) includable in the husband's estate but would qualify for the marital for US citizen spouses. There would be no Federal Gift Taxes due.

Wife Dies: simply name a new beneficiary.

*Annuitant Driven Contract

Death of the husband:
Wife has 4 options:
1) She can take a lump sum $500k Defer distributions up to 5 yrs (some companies will allow for equal distributions over the 5 years with taxes due upon each distribution)
2) Annuitize $500k within one year
3) Continue the contract in her name and name new beneficiary (Beware-some companies would force continuation of the contract at the $300k cash level whereas some companies would actually add $200k to the contract and allow for wife to continue the contract with $500k and some will also allow for and surrender charges to waived).

Federal Income Tax:
1) Distribution under the first three options would be taxable to wife at ordinary income tax rates on the gain ($400k)
2) Option #4 would allow the Federal Income Tax to continue to be deferred

Federal Estate Tax:
1) Wife is U.S citizen; value of contract is includable in husband's gross estate for marital deduction.

Federal Gift Tax: None

The Truth about Variable Annuities

EXAMPLE #5
*Annuitant Driven Contract

Charitable Remainder Trusts

Owner	Annuitant	Beneficiary
ICRT	Income Recipient	ICRT

ICRT = Irrevocable Charitable Remainder Trust

Death of Annuitant:
    ICRT options:
        1) Take a lump sum of the enhanced death benefit ($500k)
        2) Defer distribution up to 5 years

Federal Income Tax: The ICRT is tax-exempt but the income is taxable upon distribution under CRT tax rules

Federal Estate and Gift Tax: NONE

Chapter XIV

Final Thoughts

I hope that you have been able to witness and understand the nature of annuities and how complex they can be. Obviously, there are benefits in differing situations but knowing how to take advantage of those benefits is the first step to receiving them! Being prepared to take advantage of those benefits is the key. Preparedness comes from properly setting up and structuring your annuity from the beginning. If you currently own an annuity, review it with a qualified person to assist you in making sure the benefits being paid for will be utilized in the best manner at the most optimal time! The next time you hear how bad annuities are from your TV or other media personality remember they are trying to get and keep viewers, subscribers, advertising dollars, and mostly trying to prove their value by making you believe something of value was relayed to you. Fear tactics have been around for many years. Now you know the truth!

If you are a financial planner I hope you were able to open your mind to all the possibilities that an annuity could entail for allowing your client the full potential of the annuity. The examples and illustrations provided should help you understand the benefits and pitfalls of structuring the annuity as well as the riders that can be attached to the annuity. This book hopefully provided you a great starting point or a refresher on the subject of variable annuities.

NOTES

NOTES

NOTES

NOTES

The Truth about Variable Annuities